Presenting

OpUS

Bound TEXT/UREs

Volume 1: 2013 – 2015

eF[r]I(e)NDs SERIES

an OxPRESS Illustrated Anthology

TEXT/UREs (only)

©

2015

OtoPRESS

Compelled to make

·Fine Art Prints and Books·

Word

It is my pleasure–my relief, really–to at long last present the following fortuitous array of text poets and picture makers who have allowed me the liberty to present or montage, like arranged marriages, all of whom were my Facebook Friends at one time or another between the two date-ranges of April 20th through May 21st, 2013; and April 20th through September 12th, 2015, when this "montagerie" – this *hierogamos*, serialized into a passion play in twelve acts – was composed.

To those who still "follow," I am humbled; to those who left the reservation, happy trails.

~Mike Castro, Publisher, OpPRESS

This & following 3 "Abstract" paintings © by comics-artist Eric Knisley.

eF[r]I(e)NDs

eFbook OpUS of Friends, FINDs, and Fiends

How the "Found" TEXT/UREs became the "Bound" TEXT/UREs

"Op" is for optical as well as operational. What finds us, binds us. In the spring of 2013, the illusion that bound my world was losing its hold as my leading lady, an ephemeral flower, began to unspool from the reel, frame by frame, a little further out as she slept more each day. While she dreamt of cures and elixirs, I scanned The Cloud...

On an impulse, for a breather one night I began flipping thru my Facebook Friends' Photos. One of my newer "friends" – we'd never met, but I liked an opinion posted about the decline of publishing-as-industry – had scans of some of his newly photomontaged and visual poems displayed on his account that reminded me ("hello...funk soul brother...") of earlier work I had created and had mailed color prints of to (from Los Angeles back in the last days of Y2K while long-distance courting) my future wife just outside of Tampa, Florida, where we married and set up house in Year One of a New Millennium.

I asked AD Hitchin, from (at the time) Chelmsford, Essex, if he'd allow me to share his "found" images on my publisher's group site, OpPRESS. They are here bound as a First Series on pages 8 thru 12.

Three days after posting, another new "Facefriend," – again, never met, but were both just published in the same *1/25 Magazine* issue that Craig Scott hand stapled, 25 copies, every ish, and mailed out of New Jersey for a song, so from that and kindred mail-box drops (seemingly from the clouds) I had been recruiting new Friends by sending online requests to each imprint's contributors all lined up by one OCD visionary type or another like M&Ms – Neila Mezynski from Campbell, California, posted me on OpPRESS, '...do you accept prose poems? can i try to get in on that whole, *fi(e)nd of the week* thing?"

Thus *OpUS* is here born. Organic.

eMCee, September 12th, 2015

Happy Birthday, Baby

First Series: Old School/New School

First Shared by   **Mike Castro** →   **AD Hitchin**

on **OpPRESS** April 20th 2013

group

site:

www.facebook.com/OpPLEXUS

LYNCEAN OIL

Till your

ogle orbs roll

i nub you

mordant myrrh

curry and mars

juice a la goose

to,get,her

clued in batter

ease off throttle

spin sigh

cull in

doe

lint

lea

© mpcAstro '98

Proxy

Bacchus

barbiturates

gossamer

ghost

-proxy-

sylph

suffragette

the

blendblur

of

solid

objects

curb staggered
hotguns pump!
pump!
evening unshaven
clawing

consensus
the death of ballpoint
the d substitute
substitute

sky rib!
n rib!

plaster
gouged, injured
sharp lights plaster knife wou
blemish
amber
knife
in sile
mental
blood-laced
corrug

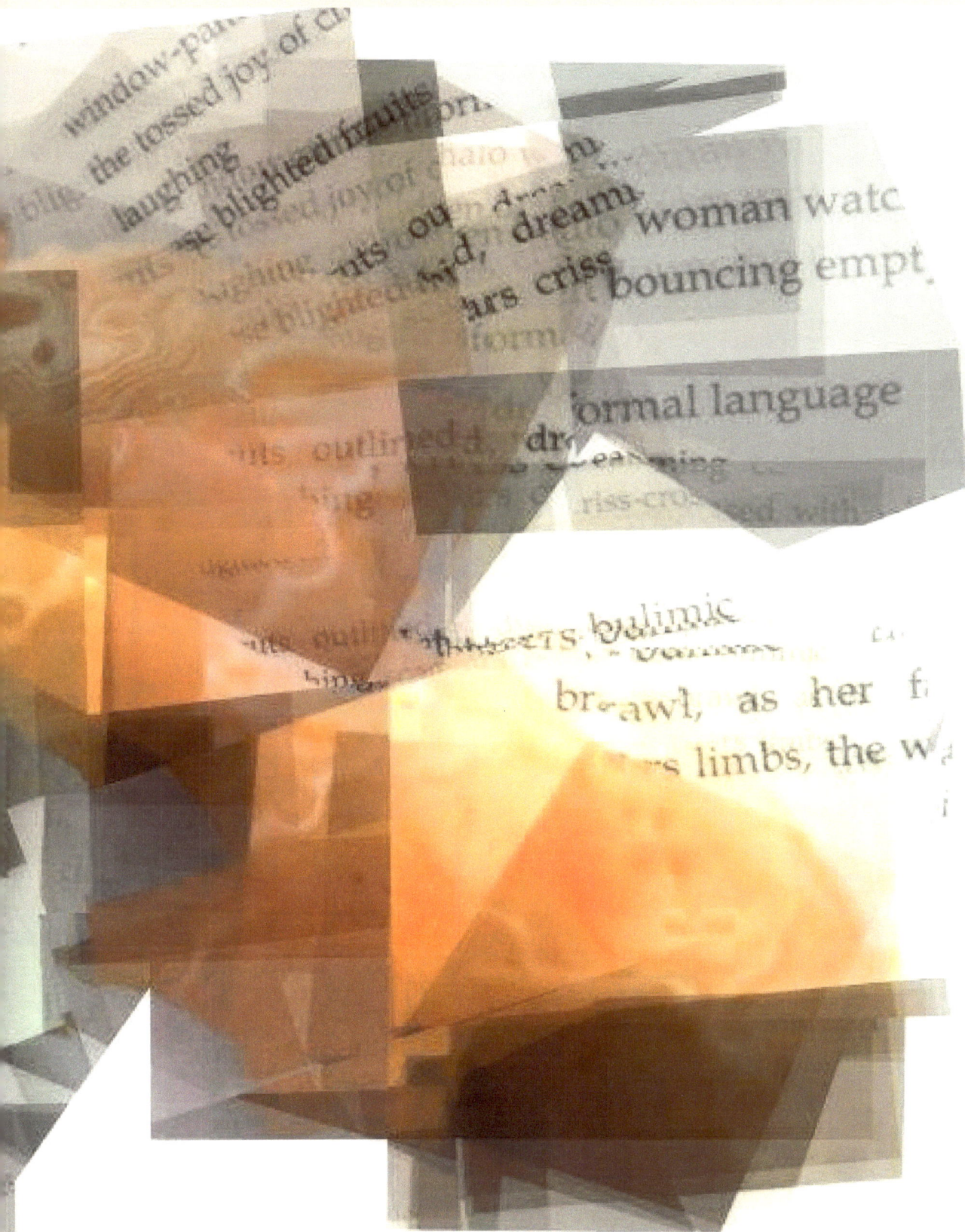

"God Worm" © 2013 AD Hitchin

The Executioner

feverkiss

nippleglow

phallusphinx

hoodwink

N
E
I
L
A
② →
M
E
Z
Y
N
S
K
I © →

WANDERIN

Sometime sometime, when she know what. It is. Happy like that.
Silver. Quiet.
Squeak. Plenty shiny sound in time before. What. Explore she will.
Hanging chair is loud. Gold. Or else applicable. Pile up heap of chair
or tire, wondering why. A fact you find loud/quiet intermittent
within/without. She' ll solve the mystery. Do.

←Belle

IMPATIENCE

Extremely beautiful, it say. Pink, red orange life saving, too. Not
her. A detriment to some. Them young old too. Bee sting. Vomit. Depend
on soil. Nice sweet smell. Too. Dry. Her. Lubricate. Huge. Enough.
Pink need moist, soil. Do is does don't. Her. Rich in touch-me-not.
Never deserve. Let her do just enough, damage. Control none. Like her
bad earth. Flower.

Study for 0

3rd Series

THE DAY VAN GOGH DIED

by Catfish McDaris

ILLUSTRATED BY

Frank Alan Bella

Chapbooked as suggested in 2004 by New Mexican outlaw poet Todd Moore.

I never planned to leave
the same day as Vincent
at least they laid him
on a pool table

It just kind of happens
that way sometimes like
an expired parking meter
that ran out of fifty cent
coins or fifty years
of solitude

I just didn't care anymore
I turned fifty years old
I chugged four cans of beer
and guzzled a bottle of wine
the wine tasted better
than the beer

Then I choked and gagged down
a full bottle of Ambien
a full bottle of Xanax
a full bottle of Remeron
and a full bottle of Clonazepam

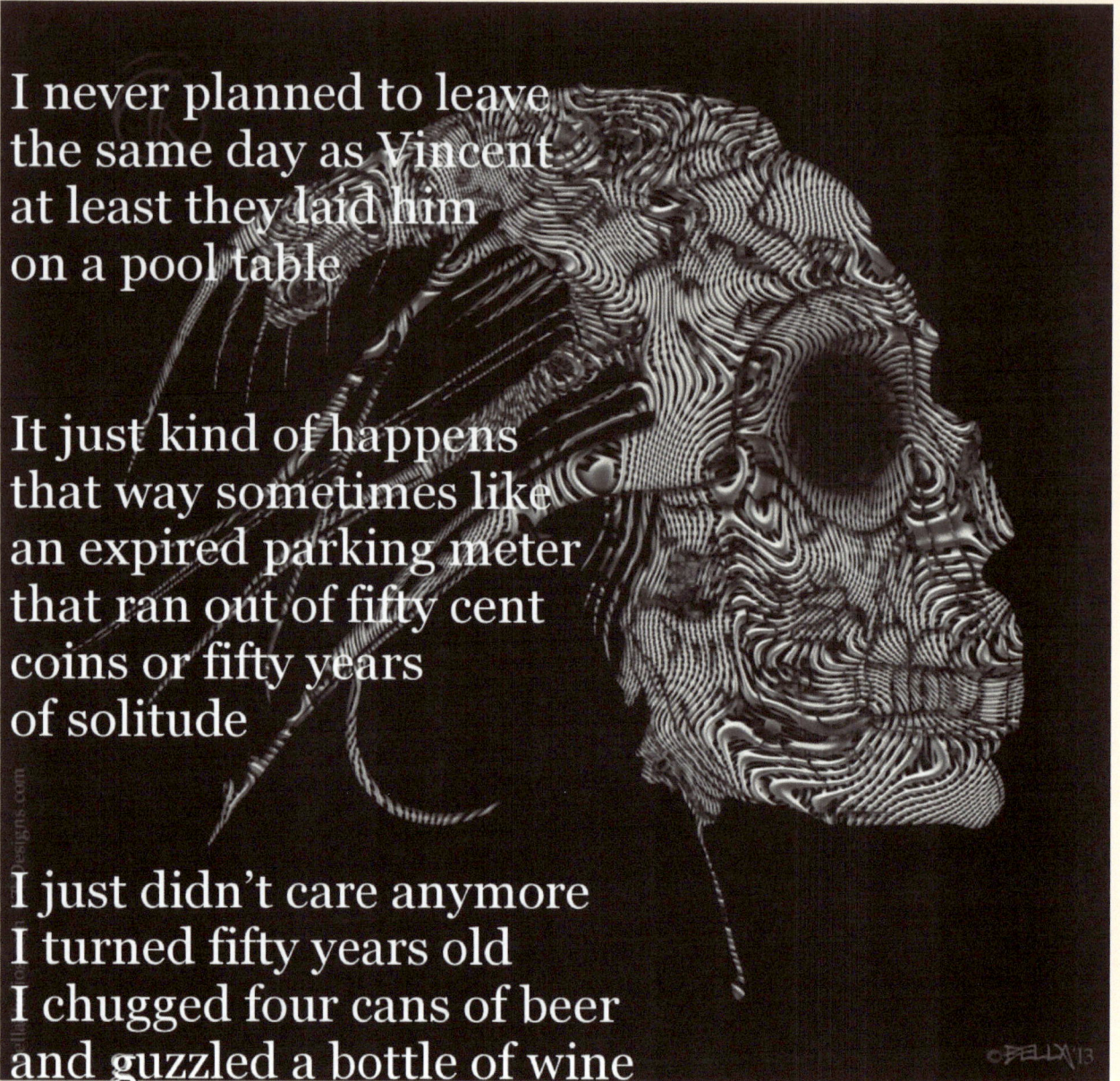

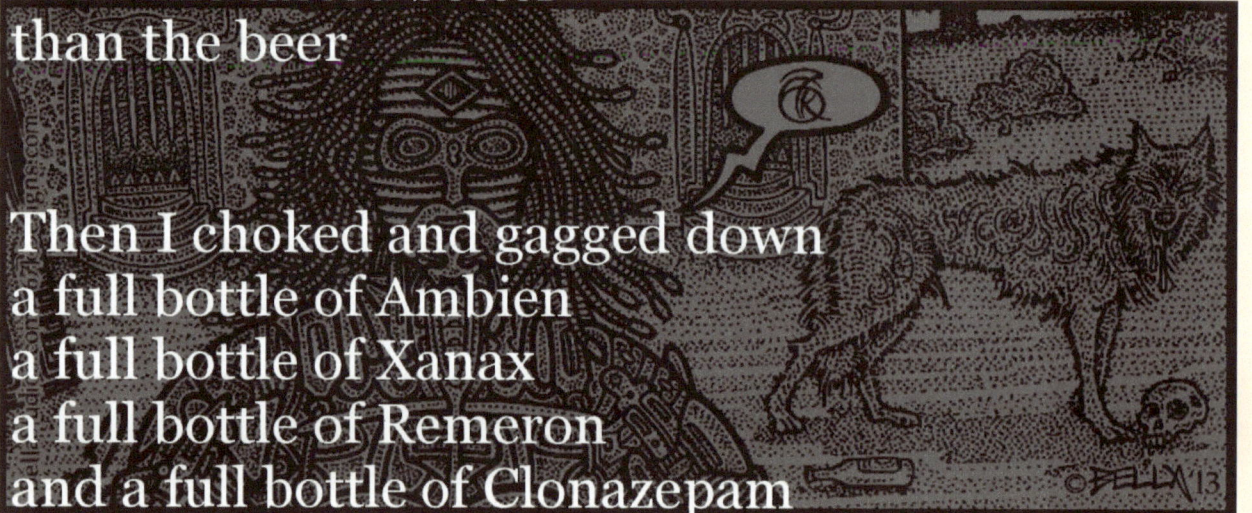

16

The beer and wine tasted
a hell of a lot better
than all those pills

Then I sat on the toilet
and waited to die but
plans don't always work
the way you want them to

My wife found me
drooling and foaming
like a rabid dog

She called 911 and the shit
hit the proverbial fan
firemen cops and paramedics
yanked me off the throne
and started stuffing nasty
ass coal down my throat

They dragged me to an
ambulance and hauled ass
to a hospital

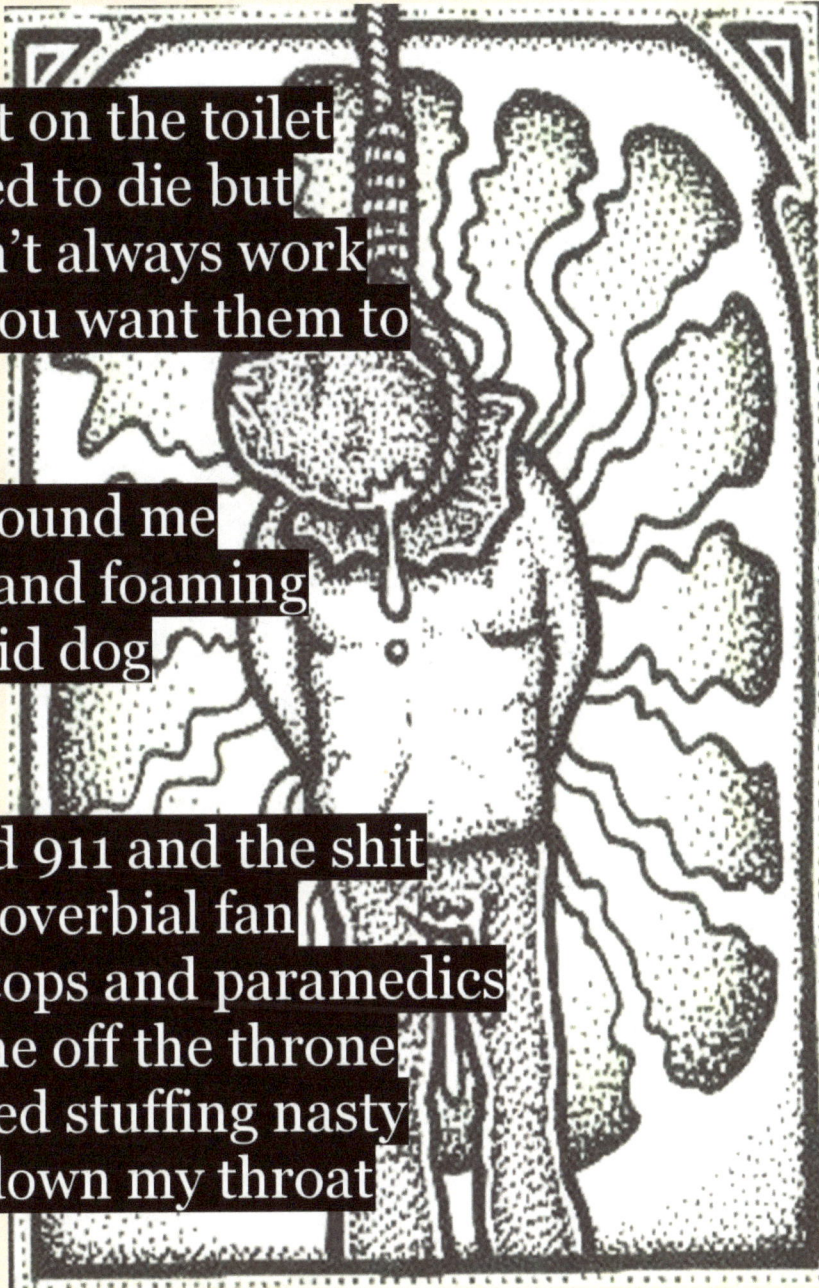

Black was coming out
of both ends of me so
fast I resembled a tube
of grease that someone
stomped on

A few hours later I was
taken to the nut house I
felt like a character in
that Ken Kesey movie only
we weren't going to see
the World Series

Two fat laughing nurses
stripped me naked hosed
me down then doused me
from head to toe with
delousing powder then
jammed a needle under the
skin of my left arm to check
for TB it later tested positive

All fucking night lunatics danced
screamed cried whined drooled
and threw feces at each other

18

The good thing was I
wasn't puking black
only defecating it
by the quart

On the third day after
I decided to pull the plug
I looked out the window and
saw a rat eating a rotten apple

A worm was attempting to
slither from a hole in
the apple it reminded
me of myself

Then another ambulance came
and took me to a different
nut house it reminded me
of the Holiday Inn

As soon as I reached my
room a guard took a look
up my ass for dangerous
paraphernalia all he saw
was black assed yellow
powder stained underwear

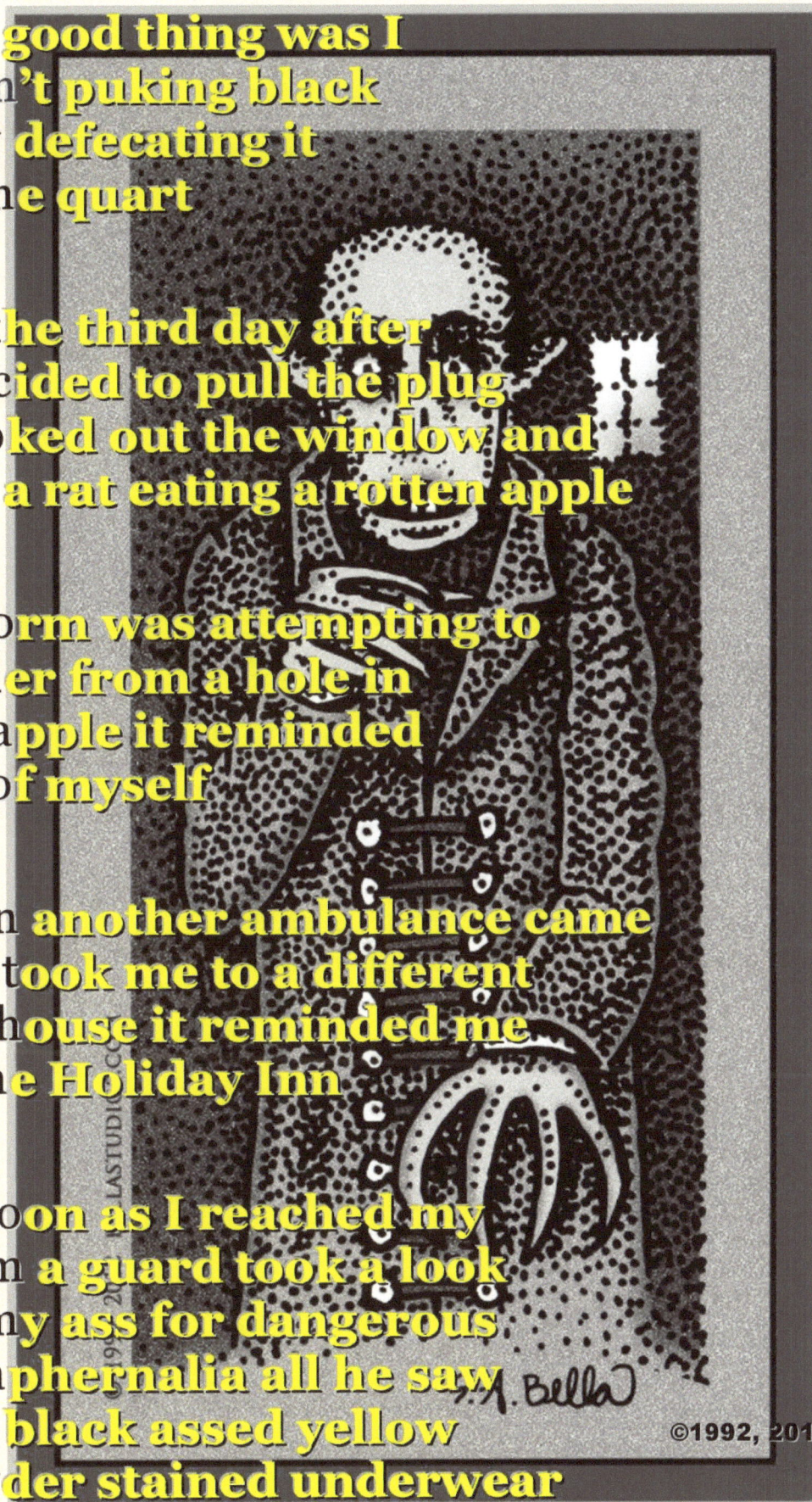

©1992, 2012

After I filled out a stack
of papers and had my belt
and shoelaces removed so
I couldn't hang myself I
checked out the contents
of my room that overlooked
the police station

There were two beds
with rubber sheets and
rubber pillows in case
you were so nuts you
couldn't make it
to the bathroom

On the beds were two
sheets of paper I'm
writing this on one now
they read Attention Patients
and Visitors This bed has been
cleaned and prepared for the
next patient Please do NOT sit
or place your belongings on the
bed If you need help please
contact a staff member It didn't
have anything on them about writing
on them so I guess long rambling
poems are cool

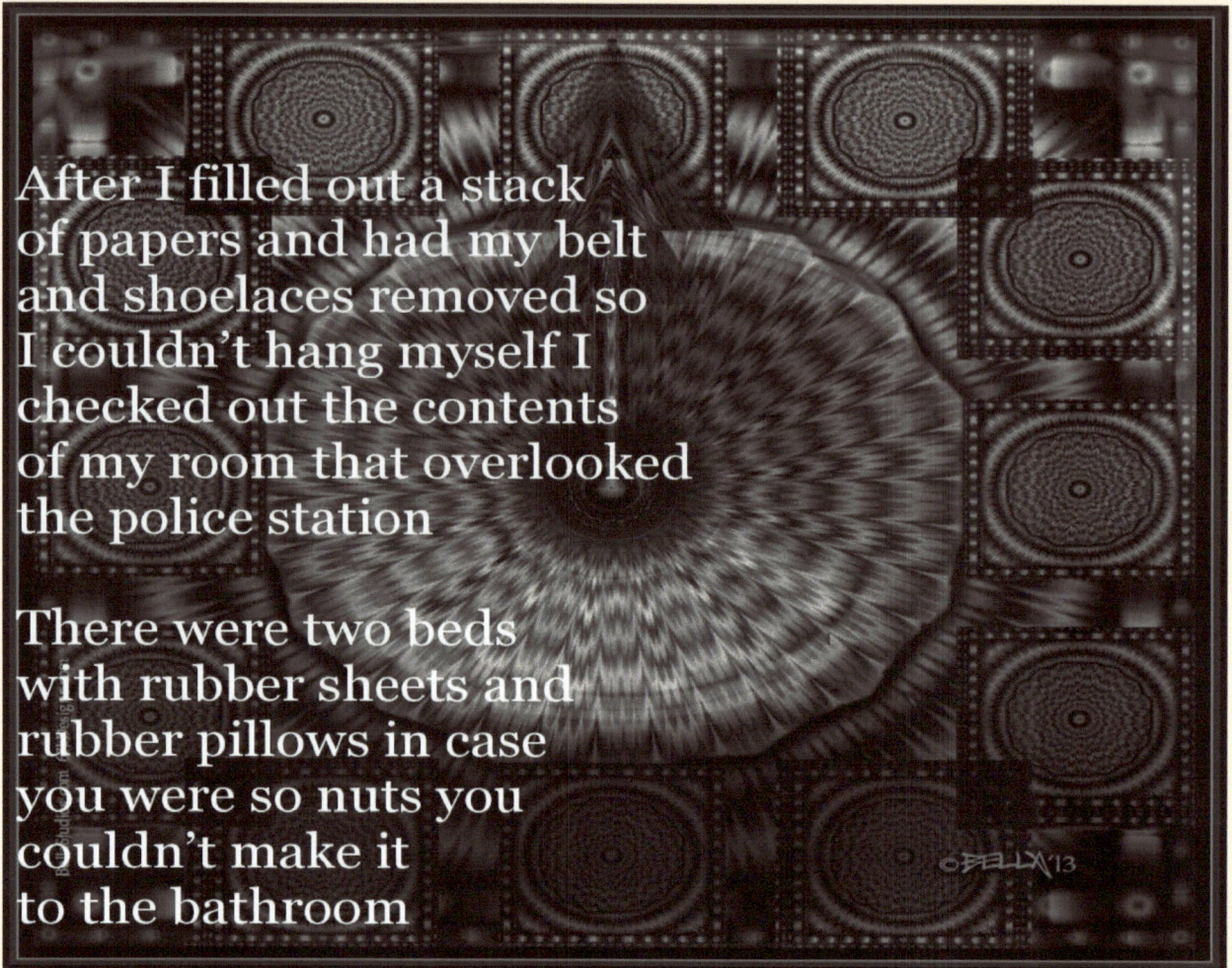

In a small pink plastic wash pan
were two tiny bars of soap with
Bob Barker's name on them there
was also a tube of roll on deodorant
called Bob Barker MAXIMUM SECURITY

I took a shower trying the products
I sure as shit didn't feel clean or
remotely MAXIMUM SECURE

I felt like that old white
headed crust on television
that for decades has been
reaming rubes with trips
cars and furniture

I felt like going to
The Price Is Right Show
and coming on down
the aisle to stone Bob with
his worthshit products

By now everyone is asleep
so I asked the nurse for
a sedative to help me sleep
I'd been taking them for twenty
years of course not entire
bottles at a time

The nurse had orders not
to give me any drugs so
sleep was out of the scenario

I thought about carving
a gun like John Dillinger
did but I had no knife

Besides the fucking Bob
Barker soap wasn't big
enough to make into a
decent derringer so I
looked out into the night
and disappeared inside myself

poem © 2004 Catfish McDaris
private profile photo of Catfish McDaris—somewhere—and amigos dipped in acid
born July 29, – *the Day van Gogh died* – 1953, 100 years after his patron saint was
born who then later died of a bullet to the chest in 1890, July 29th, a messed up day

All remaining 12
illustrations©1990–2013 Frank Alan Bella

picotopoem: Reprinted with permissions as an Original TEXT/URE by O PRESS

Cinco de Mayo, 2013

Footsteps Brother!

4th Series: Home Is a Circle

I still have trouble at my mother's death.
All I saw was a body with blue feet.
Her eyes were open and her mouth did
Not speak.   My numbness
Knew no time.   I remember massaging
Her feet the night before. And the night
Before that, I watched   Close Encounters of
The Third Kind.   A boat lay on its side
In Mongolia.   I had sunk my fourth
Can of beer while Dreyfuss
Carved his mystic mountain of
Potato mash.
I was getting drunk while my mother
Was getting dying.
Bruised and battered, body born
To die, to taste the fire on my tongue.
If the water was clear enough
If the water was still enough
Perhaps I could have seen
The warning sounds of your milked
Dying breast.
That night I cried to the wind and
Sleep.
Footsteps before the October dawn,
Brother, brother, our mother has died!

12 pages illuminated by **Sibylle Schwarz**   ← © ↘
                        for 18 poems by **Ken Trimble**

The Carpenter.

**God
is
an
empty
chair.**

Waiting.

**Have we ever arrived?
We are still waiting
at the station.
Waiting for
a train.**

Home.

**When I was
a child
I imagined
I could see tiny
bubbles of air
dancing
in front of me
as the train
crossed
the stinking
river
to my
childhood
home.**

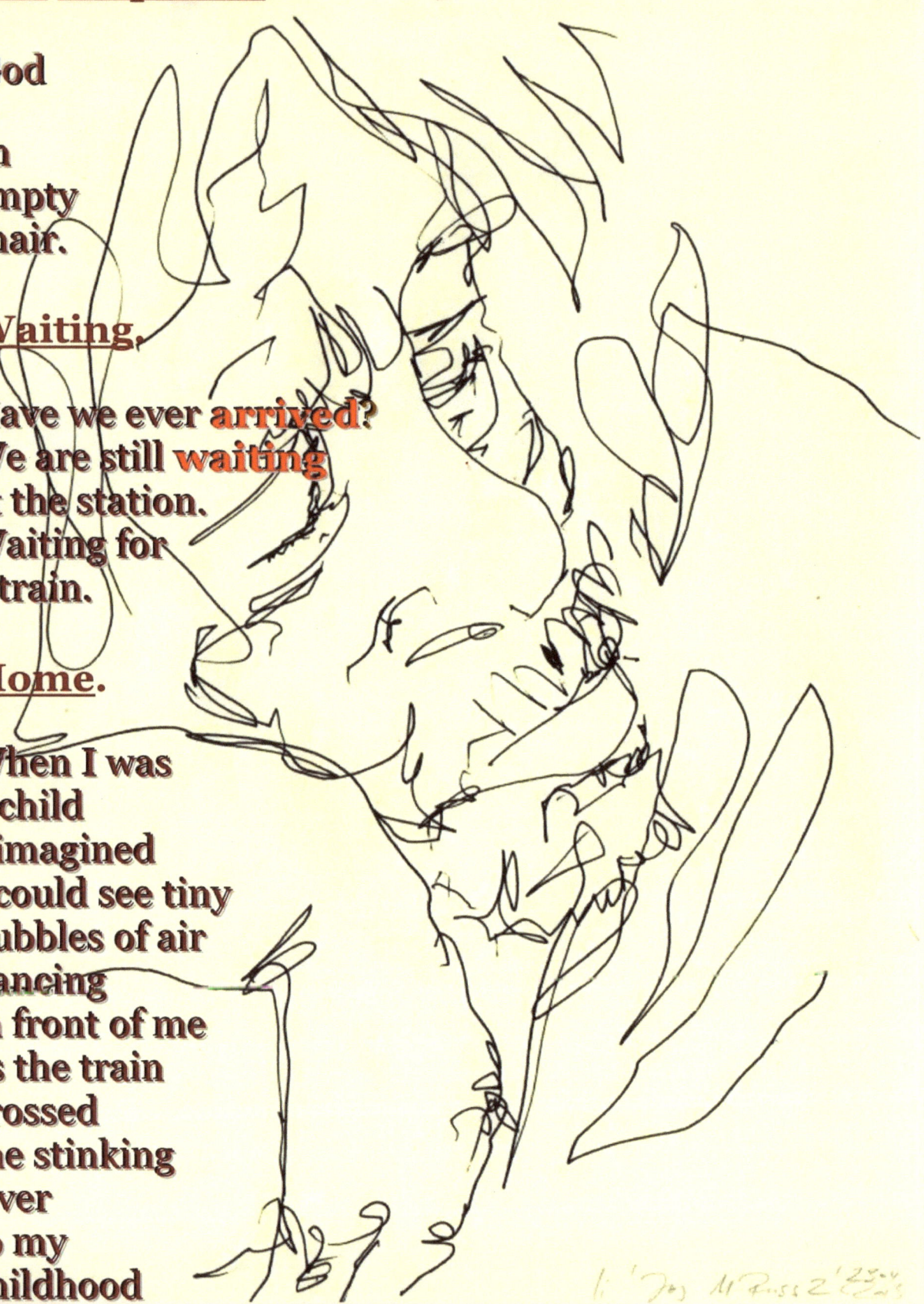

24

Life.
It is not so much the camera
nor the person
controlling that creates.
It is beyond
all of this.
To see with the eye
is to know
without knowing.
It is passive awareness
that awakens the soul,
before even the light
has struck!

One Word.
One day I will find simple words
to tell you how I feel
so you can know in your heart
the clarity of my seeing
and the truth
of my
knowing.

Free.
Just because I'm a touch mad,
a bit loopy,
a bit around the bend,
mad as a loon haunting
the wild marshes
of our city streets;
doesn't mean
we can't
be friends.

Wolves.

My uncle, the shaman of Williamstown
wore a magpie's eye,
and danced with the wolf spiders.
He was a lunar expeditionary,
an opiate connoisseur
of fine drugs.
A master of lunacy,
my teacher of madness.
My uncle was a tripper,
an insane weaver
of words,
charging the inner
depths
of my crazy
soul.

Child of God.

You think you can mould me from some piece of clay
into something similar to your self.
You want me to swim in the same ocean
fly in the same air
I am not some piece of stone
to be sculpted
a blank canvas to be painted
We are as different
as the sun and the moon
I am not
your
child
of God.

26

<u>Secret</u> <u>Corridors</u>.

I am I
not you.
Forgetting, things I do not see;
who at times I manage to visit when walking.
A memory, held a moment; no more,
then, dashed like the wind; gone.
I am I
not you.
Who sits at his desk typing words.
Who feels the presence of the rippling
quiet.............. .
Who craves the silent roar.
I am I
not you.
A secret corridor where prayers exist,
and a shelter for the birds; who are
holes in heaven
for us to pass.
I am I
not you.
A howling madman of blinded sorrow
who dwells in dreams,
and nightmares of cathedral bells struck,
my kingdom for a drink, I cry!

<u>Words</u> <u>Falling.</u>

Poets:
We
are
the
crazy
bastards
of
Homer
and
Catullus.

The
Catullus
of
the
racetrack.
The
Homer
of
Springfield.

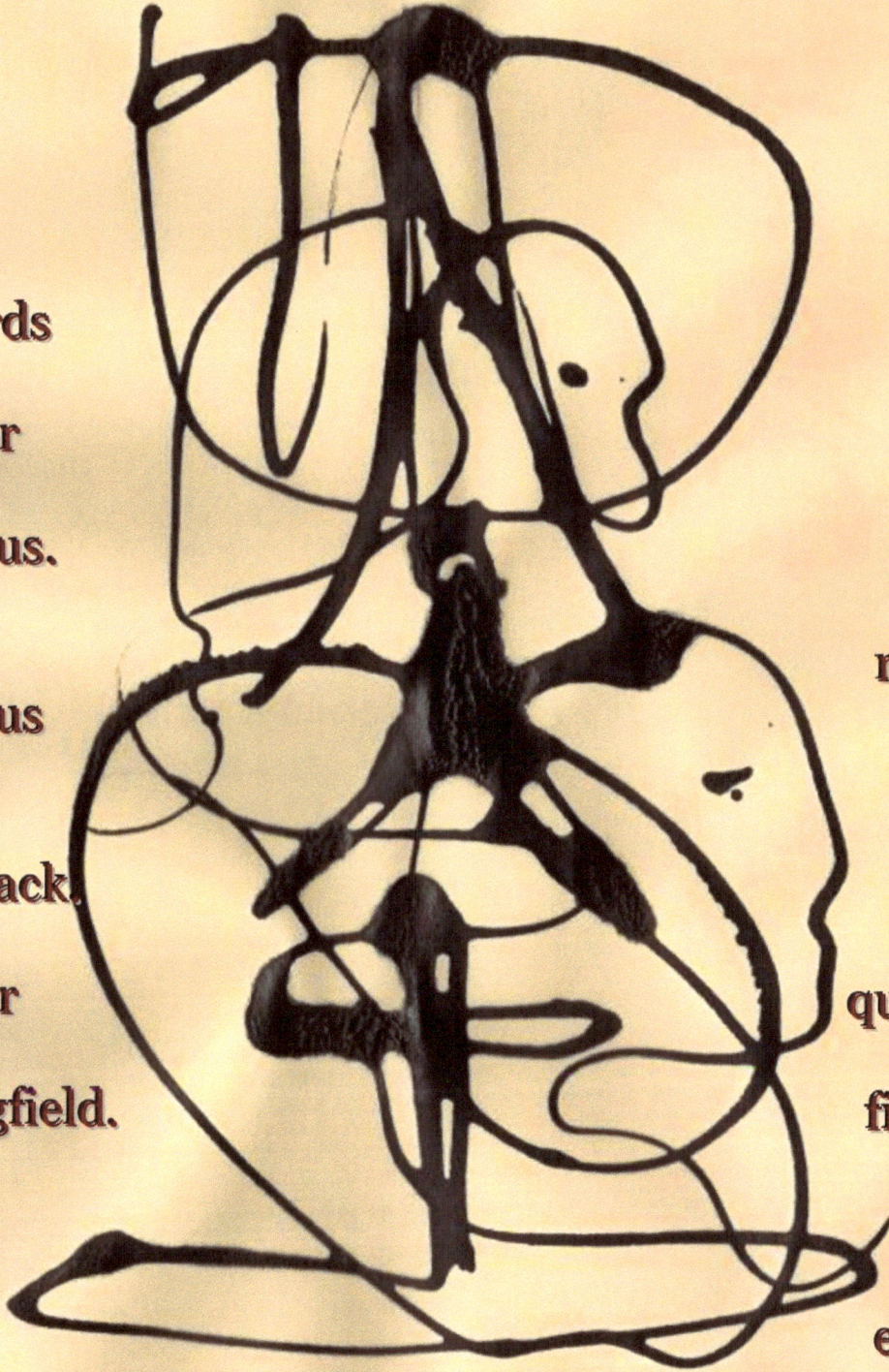

Poets:
We
are
the
words
of
verse
falling
on
to
the
rooftops
of
Prague.

Always
leaving
questions,
never
finishing
our
poems;

enigmas
to
the
end.

Murray Street.

Norm wore a boiler suit and carried a gun.
Steve sang the gospels, recited his rosary,
talked in his Latin and danced like a monkey
on a bender.
Brian drank his beer 6am long neck in the kitchen.
He told us stories of his prison days at Barwon
laughing mad, foaming at the mouth.
Young Billy sang Frank Sinatra badly in the night.
A wanna be wanna be.
Big Wendell was a rag and bone man
wandering through the streets
looking for his man.
Sweet Mary Lou moaned like a wildcat in the room
next to mine leaving her g-strings in the shower.
And I, well I drank cardboard wine... morning,
day, and night.

Johnny Boy.

Johnny Boy lived next to the boiler room,
his room was full with newspapers
going back a year or two.

He smoked like a goddamn train.
He wore a goaty beard
all shiny with blackboot polish.

He told me his son was an airline pilot
and one day he would
take him outta there
some day.

<u>El Duende</u>.*

My soul
yearns
for
the song
of the
sea.

To swim
into the
depths
so
I can
hear
those
black
sounds
singing
in my
heart.

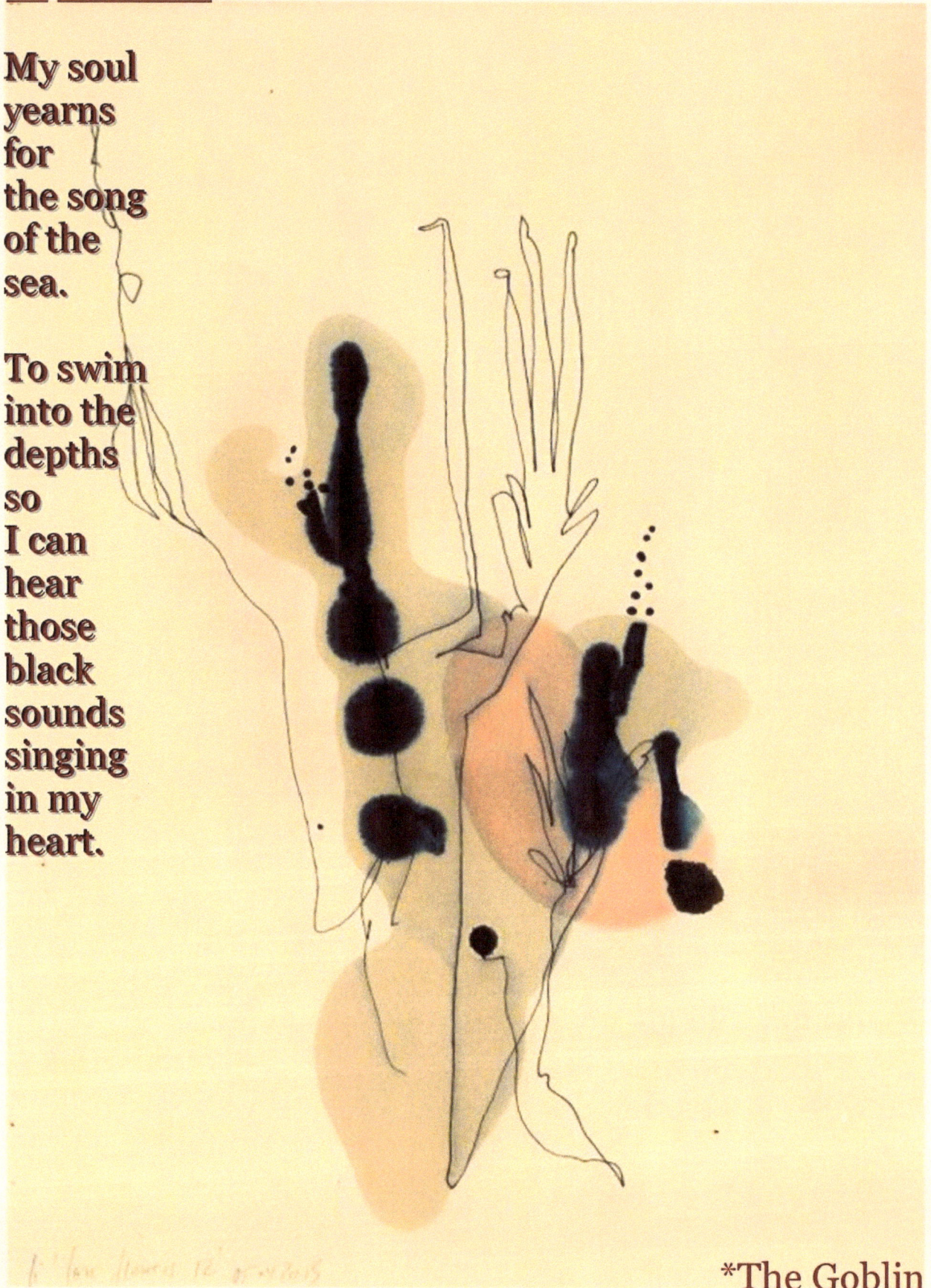

*The Goblin

<u>Indian</u> <u>Night</u>.

I lived among snakes and scorpions
spiders on the mesh
a bat hugging the walls
mighty grasshopper looking at me
all things well.....
I heard prayers morning evening night
I drank Old Monk with friends
Sannyasins arrive by the bullock cart
I am smoking the Indian night
down by the sacred river.

The Hermit.

Silent waters
yellow moon
mountain mist
and deer on the run.
Prayer mat and beer
Which will I have first?
Drifting silence and wet afternoons
I think I'll read Kerouac
perhaps St. Augustine
the black.
Lonely sun
tired days
friends come around.

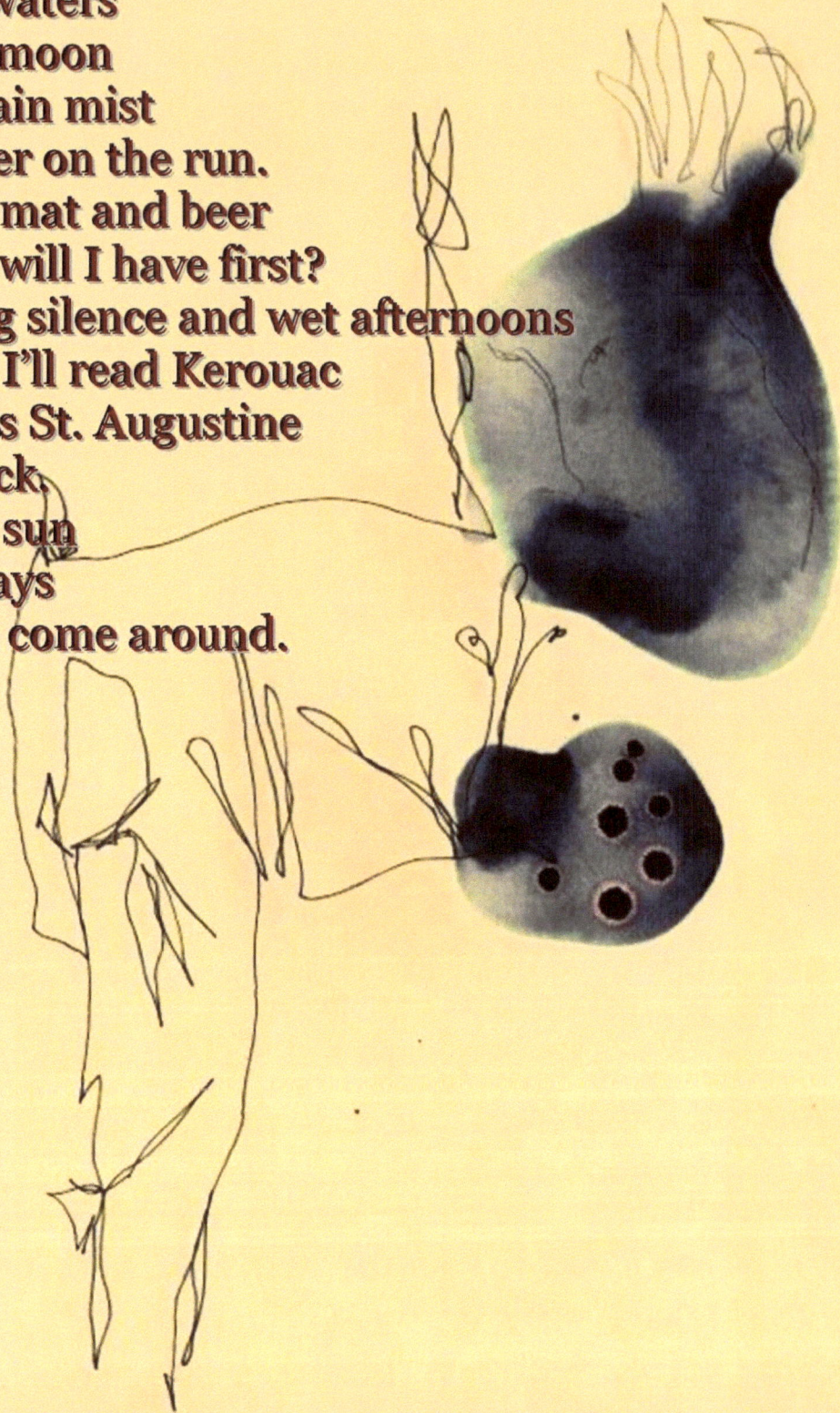

Bodhisattva Baby.

Ten thousand
things on
this earth.
The Buddha's
and
Bodhisattva's.
Ten thousand
promises
of
the
road.
Ten thousand
things
all in this earth
are
grasping
hold
of emptiness.
There's
nothing
more
to say.

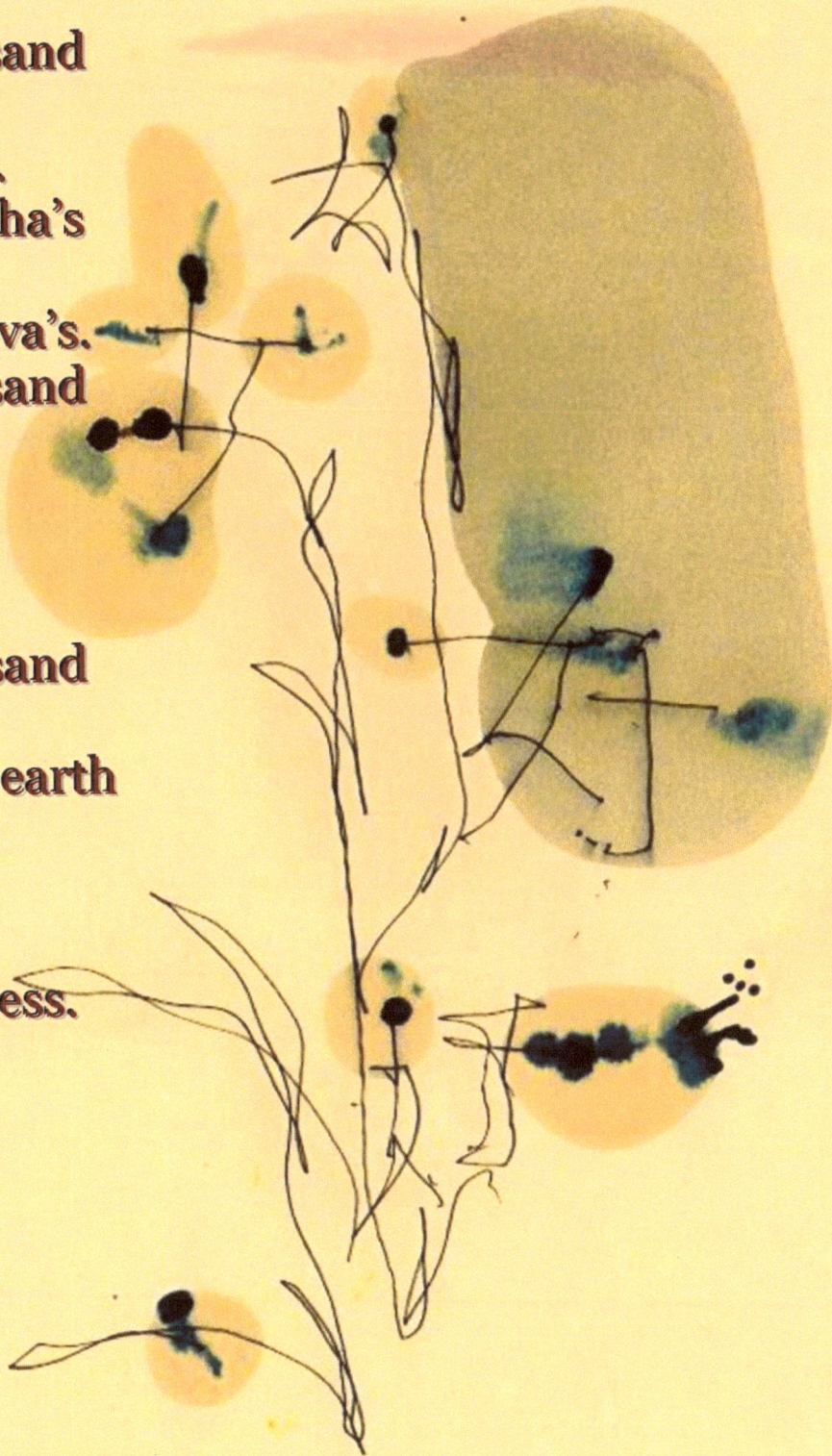

Cold, cold ground.

Lay me down in the
Cold, cold ground.
Sing hallelujah
Sing glory be.
The farm's going down
The bank called in.
No need to wake.
Life's in the bin.
Got me a bottle.
Got me a gun.
Got me Tom Waits
Singing the cold,
Cold ground.

This 4th Series first posted online May 21st, 2013.

'the dancer 23' Wednesday note' 25·04·13

23-month *OpUS* Interruptus after Erin turned from green to gold to *Go Baugh* in her sleep, June 6th - 7th, 2013.

SET

5th Series Reboot, Apr 20, '15; 2yrs aft 1st

ETRINITY

Triptych by

ErinColleenCastrO

THE THREE WISE MEN

Tribute

EXCERPTED from
"The Circle" by
Mike Castro

NET

Her spurts of energy lasted maybe one to a few days, from an hour to sometimes all afternoon each day. And then her fibromyalgia would flair up and she'd be bedridden for twice as many days she was up. Then I'd ask her to take it easy for another day or so. Sometimes a week or two would pass before she'd go back to the canvas. One day I came around the partition that separated my desk from her studio, and canvas was draped with an old bed sheet. She didn't want it to be seen until it was done. Then some weeks later I'd come bobbing up for air to make us dinner—your daddy's *hep*; he knows what cooks—to be shortstopped by a lying-in-wait unveiling. Sort of primitive surreal, with layered, broad, flat sections, mostly. But intriguing. Yellow, red and orange against a green background, if I recall, reminiscent of Frida Kahlo's hospital bed portrait with IV tubes—except abstracted into Erin's own style: a distressed meat casing seated, bent at the waist against a table, entangled with these thick tubes she'd call "connections." A local gallery operator who had been showing my prints came by with her 7-year old son because Erin had been pining for her own grandmunchkins ensconced somewhere over the rainbow. Daphne praised Erin's first ever painting. Later, my wife asked if I really liked it. I suggested she needed to touch up some feathered edges, was all, and then it should be done.

The next day it was all re-layered over in black. Solid. Like a mudslide of tar opium paved over a chocolate depression. I was stunned. Why? I asked. "You said you didn't like it." Baby, I cried, I just told you to touch it up and it'd be perfect. Daphne, yesterday, told you she was impressed. Didn't you believe us? "Mike, are you in love with Daphne?" Oh baby. Autonomic Automan, your dilated pupils and flush pulse betray you. But, in hindsight, I think when I imagined her pictograms knocking on Void's door; she rewrote the plot into an airlock blowing its hatch out into the calculus of my diamond-star predictions, with a wink to their First Assumption: If everything touches, there is no space.

The shale and shellac background paints became a night sky with a black hole backdropping a venous "flashtree of lightning," fronting white, pink and red stars, with an aerial flame streaking. She called it, "Catch a Falling Star." I knew that the limb/bolt "connections" were my promised neuromantic net. She was the meteor to be caught. She was falling. Her hands were too swollen from too many streaks across the canvas, so she asked if I'd sign it for her. All of her finer brushes were frazzled from her broad-stroke technique, so I signed it with a toothpick, ECCO '12. Ecco is also the Latin interjection for "Here! Here I am!"

She completed two more, each in its own idiom, yet all telling her story as a triptych. She painted the ending first. Next was the middle, the present, about her relationship with her daughter going on four years fallow, tho' that hadn't occurred to me until the day Erin's mother and father, Lois Jean and Jon from California, phoned; mom on extension, a week after Erin ran out of current. I named the middle piece—I asked her by then to let me name them after signing —, "The Three Wise Men," a painting of 3 fantastical trees, each unique and otherworldly. The middle acrylic was the largest, centered by a meta-apple tree with red heart-shaped fruits. Beneath that tree, with rubyfruit dropping to the ground,

was a lone white bird, sort of a duck tailed dove with goulashes for legs. I joked that if the trees were the Magi, then the duck must be Jesus. She liked the title, tho', and it also intrigued her mom. So, between tears, L.J. asked me to describe again ECCO's "trees painting." *And then it came* to me... The Forbidden Fruit Tree was E's daughter hoarding hearts, pushing "Nana" away from the two saplings on either side. The grandson, Michael (my namesake) *was then* obvious to me on the left, sturdy and *full of loud* colors. And her granddaughter, Ashley, *on the* right, was a milky tangle of sleek *translucent* tubes. Erin had been nicknamed Tweetie by an a

cappella chorus she was a member of before I uprooted from Venice West to transplant myself east. Eden's gate held open by a sun-bright canary trilling to end up milling for a heart from a turned-bitterroot daughter to drop haw on downy head come hell or high water—so the goulashes.

The omega of the triptych I intuitively ordered as the alpha of the grouping. She was very mystical and corpora obscura would visit her often. She also was adept at keeping a door open between our dreams, so breakfasts were times to compare notes, which is how I fathomed this finalé to really be the prelude... a scene of two enormous waves approaching a deserted, powdered sugar (silica) beach with a thick yellow sun in a burning raspberry sky. Every color was a solid, autonomous region vaguely reminiscent of fauvist Gauguin. Depopulated of nudes or totems. Deserted. I joked that I'll name it "Spumoni" because of the gay ice cream sky and, even though yellow, a pistachio planted sun: a nod to her Italian on her mother's side. We agreed, tho', on "Abandon," because that's the ghost it evoked. But I'd sometimes joke over the weeks that maybe "Spumoni" would be better. Then one day, she started adding an extra wave as some breakwater. I couldn't believe it. I knee jerked and said, Hey! I already signed ECCO '13. You need to learn when to stop. She told me I needed to let her be her own artist. I wanted to kiss her; so I left her alone. I later renamed it "Set," for the waves. And then, while describing it to Lois, it's meaning, too, revealed itself... During a summer break before our junior year, when Jon wasn't allowing her to date before her 16th birthday, she let me know that her parents and she were going to camp on Doheny Beach and we arranged to meet on a certain day and time by a certain lifeguard tower. Mike Miller, who first introduced us, and I drove down I-5 that day and like a dream, there she was, 15 and string-bikinied. Me all skin and bone. Mike stood lookout for The Dad.

She and I went out swimming and got caught in a rip current. We were pulled fairly far out. Erin was about to panic but I remembered to not fight the current, to instead swim parallel with the shoreline until we were out of the deep suck. Side by side we swam out of the rip, just like the posted "Danger" said we could. And even tho' a half mile or so out that hot-as-raspberry, cloudless blue sky day, the change in current now assured us we were golden. Doheny's sand: ecru cotta. Gulf beaches here: bone crystalose. So because 33 years later I paralleled myself since with her here, she powder-sugared our memorable day.

ECCO started a 4th canvas a couple of weeks before she left me talking to myself. It's still behind me on the easel. All blue. Mostly wavy mariner below an atmo-mistic topside. Driven home from the art store, while I pulled us into the driveway, she asked what was meant by, "Paint the light." I told her to try to see all the colors of what she wanted to paint. Free the aluminum grays and lazurite greens from bark of living oak that we just parked under, for instance, with shadations of corporal-punished blue. The light tickles out color in spasms, not prisms. However, I reminded her, I really like what you've been doing so far.

$ERIE$ $Ɛx: MAGICK LOVE

pho**to mirages:** "Luc/i/us: Sex-Magick"
by **Operating Shaitan**

poe**m:** "for all I know of Love"
by **Niall Rasputin**

Put your fair flesh against mine.
Closer.
I want to breathe you in
and never exhale.

Crawl through my venial caves,
dance barefoot to the rhythm of my pulse,
slide against me;
blessed friction.
Settle into this addiction.
It's too

pure

to be

dirty.

Hide here until your demons
    fade back into the fire that warms us.

Put your bare soul against mine.
       Closer.
I want to bury my martyr face in your
               blooming curls
to dress my shame in your saving grace;
to see if my happiness
                resurrects.

Protect me from myself.
I'll protect you from the world.

Just for an infinite moment,
   until the scars fall asleep.

Until the stars
stop crying.

Just a bit closer.

This is where my True Self
   lives.

BLUE YEAR

You chased trains
Took beatings
She clung
You loved You loved You loved
Who you are
Always forever
Anger behind her eyes
like raisin oatmeal and ice water
She has moved beyond indifference
Cries when you touch her
in the blue room
You beg her to stay
She runs into the void
of not you
Not You Not You
Was it the song you didn't sing
The cigarettes you smoked
She rides buses
You chase trains
You love You love You love

peinture

© Jocelyne Desforges, 2007

TEXT © *puma perl, 1/1/11*

PARTY AT THE GOD HOUSE

Belinda's teaching Stacey to salsa

Sandy's back on a Harley

Tommy Pray lifts weights

and smokes cigarettes

Cousin Willie watches baseball

in high definition

Judy wears a red bandana

Eddie rides bareback

Jon dances like a white boy

Hector sings at my window

Jimi plays the clouds

I lie awake

like a starving dog,

waiting for an invitation

Mr. and Mrs. God

request your presence

Party at the God House

Ghosts lean against dusty cars

smoking Newports, hustling change

spilling wine for the brothers upstate

In dreams, I arrive at the party

Chelsea Hotel, Room 100

I borrow Marilyn's polka dot dress

stilettos donated by Sylvia Rivera

Just like Don Cherry, I play

a rhythm on the door,

and step over the threshold

into the light.

My eyes open.

Dogs bark.

My invitation drips blood.

The eighties took my partners

The nineties stole my lovers

I have one friend.

Her name is Ruby True.

SER❽IES

TEXT by Erie, Pennsylvania,
© poet RON ANDROLA

3 poems

eERIE EYES

pictUREs by Huddersfield, England,
© artist CHINA9

7 acrylics on canvas

WOMAN IN A LIGHT RED DRESS

Live webcam in Chicago, I'm
Dressed for sleep in another
Erie night, but before I drift:

Startling woman in a light red
Dress, a very short dress, crosses
The gallery taking pictures

Of the paintings. She appears
Like a Hiroshima symphony
Sudden, total. Her long

Dark hair, her gorgeous, soft
Face, her ass, a jackhammer
Insistence between my tubular eyes.

She disappears from the camera.

My wife coughs in our bedroom.
The woman in a light

Red, short, tight, shimmery
Dress is in her 20s, a fascinating,
Sweet, vulnerable girl. She returns

& I watch an older rich bastard pull her
Into a photo. Hooking her waist like
Meat. The flash releases his

Barbed catch.
She spins on high heels
& her arms are quick, repetitious

Wings. She's smiling
But I know the depth of her
Soul.

LET'S WAKE THE DEAD

Bang yr fists onto whatever is currently
In front of you, including air. Continue
Pounding as the beat shapes, as clouds
Thin to tongues in the blue sky. There
Are wild turkeys in the woods of upper
Pennsylvania, they splatter upwards.
We are marching no matter what no
Matter where nor why. Squeeze for
Ignition. You are a magnolia.
An electromagnetic magnolia. I am a spider
On the verge of becoming a black cat,
A purple-eyed kangaroo, a whitewashed
Emotion. With broken fingers
Type. Windows burst like cymbals
In a sandstorm,

Leaning, tensed
But short,

Reversing elongation with
One exact pin point on the rubbery world.
A continuous cupcake.
Butterflies emerge from
Melting walnuts
With wings of scissors.
Bingo. The last person.
The depth of intensity
Is painfully dark,
Of course.
The wounds of shadow,
The scars.
The yard is coffee-colored tweed.
It is soft & dangerous with dog shit.
I suggest many, many bells.
Become bells.

GOLD IN THE HILLS

→

Dinosaur bones, gold in the hills,
scrawled in z veins deep into
caves & eons. Our conversation
is layered on a highway. Crows,
old ghosts & severe black shadows
pour into us. Denver drivers
lurch & fly & rush, & we talk
about gravitating towards stability
as a life force in this undone world.
Quick brakes, the pull of speed,
3-way, 4-way, I don't really know.
Are you sleeping? This isn't
my dream without you & yr
warped intellect, the pain in the
ass of love. Get over it sarcasm
becomes you, sweetheart. Beneath
yr declarations a million
prehistoric ants eat yr ends,
ingest yr gentle adjectives.

IXth Series

There, but for the grace of god, go I

(a flash fotonovella)

poem
"Like a Thief"
© 2014
Ben John Smith,
Industrial Painter,
stealing breathers
between huffs...

cover drawing © 2011, Matthew Shaw

How quick the night comes after wine

morning-after selfie © 2013, Ben John Smith

posterized 2015 by OpPRESS

after sex
After the cat
has eaten.

On-The-Job photo, "Blue Oubliette" © 2013, Ben John Smith

How quick the night comes when it should be day

photo © 2013, Ben John Smith
posterized 2015 by OpPRESS

and the sun
as bright as her
skin

OTJ photo © 2013, Ben John Smith
posterized 2015 by OpPRESS

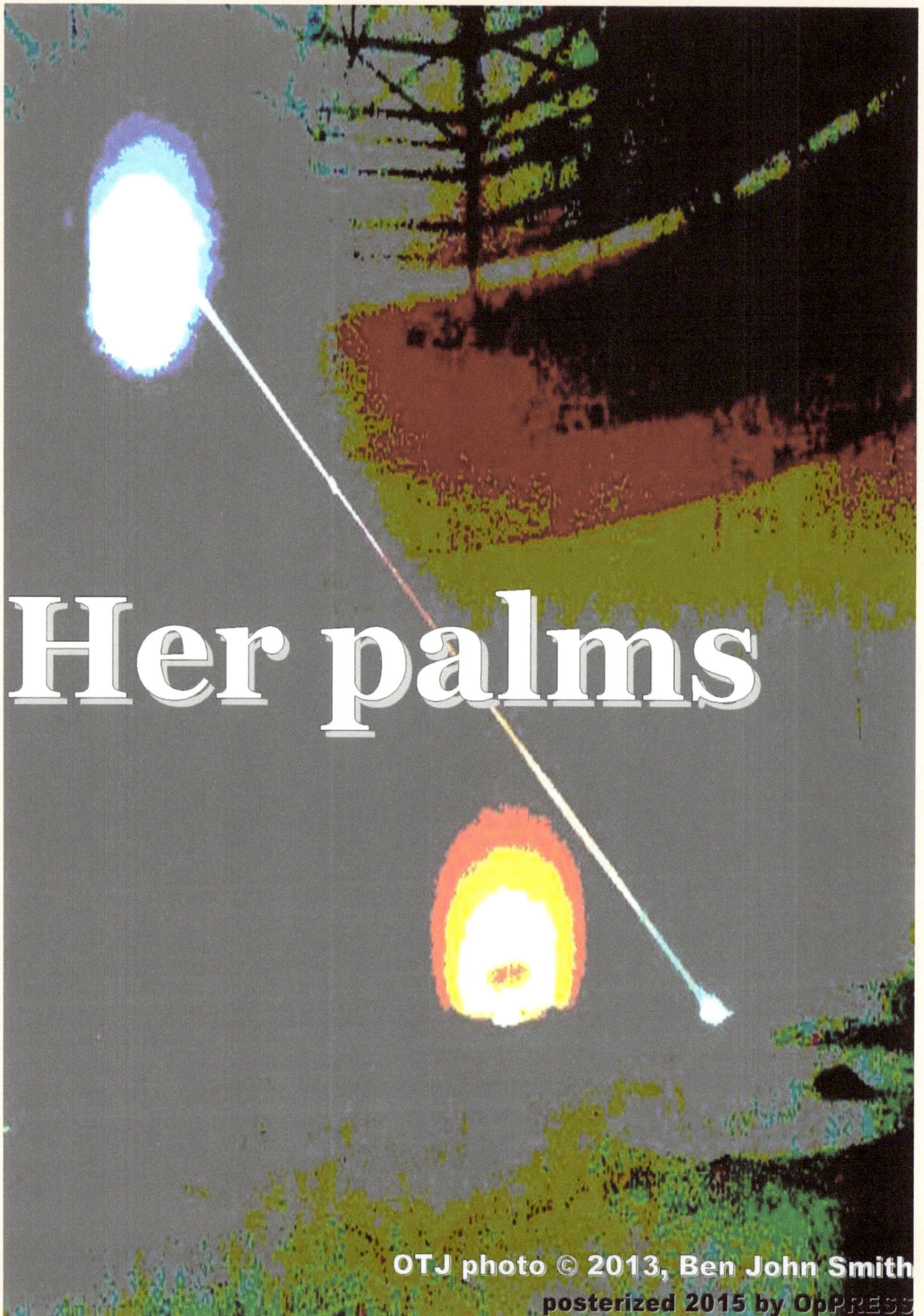

Her palms

OTJ photo © 2013, Ben John Smith
posterized 2015 by OpPRESS

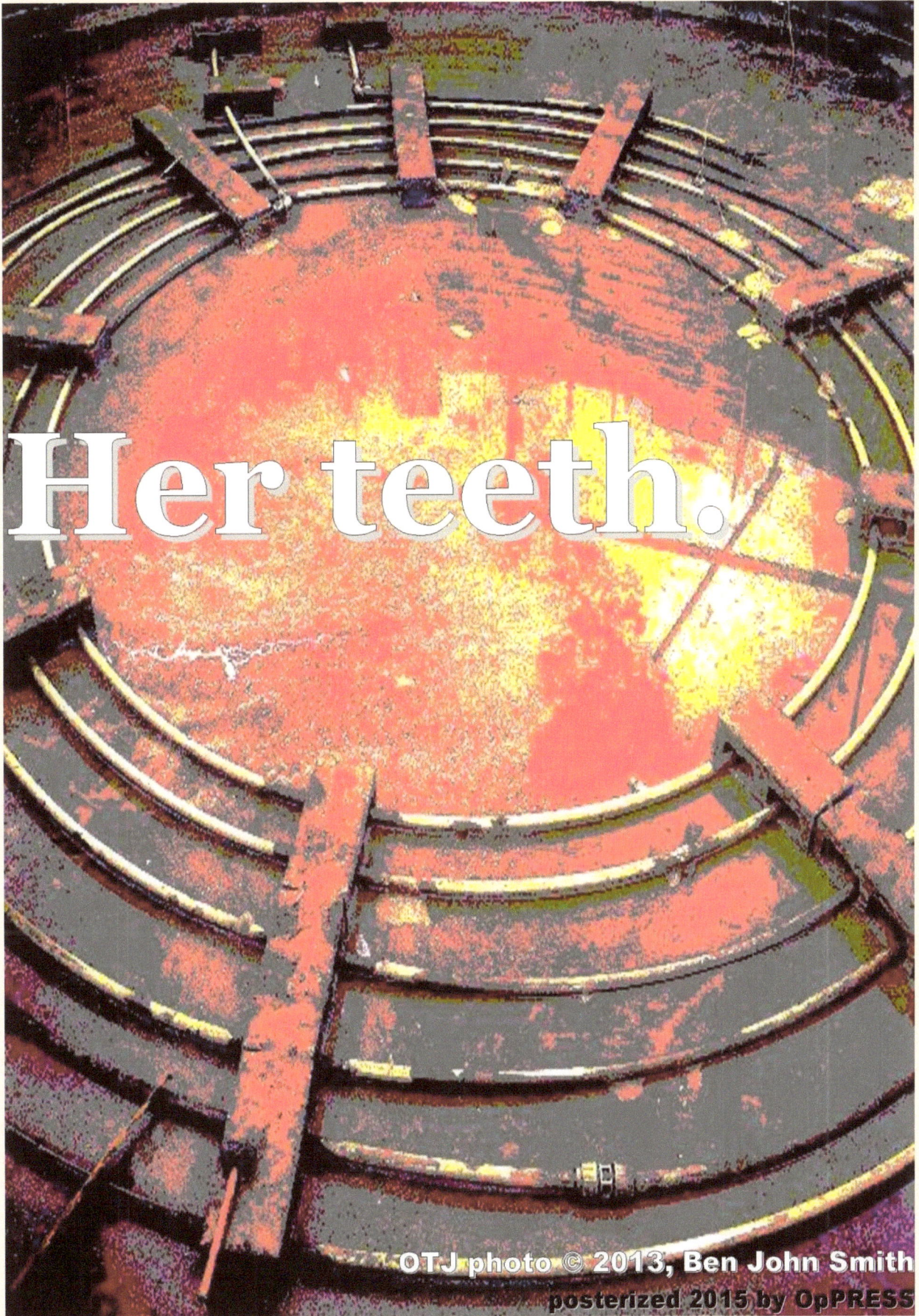

Her teeth.

OTJ photo © 2013, Ben John Smith

posterized 2015 by OpPRESS

How quick it all comes when i just want to go.

painted fotocollage © 2014, Ben John Smith

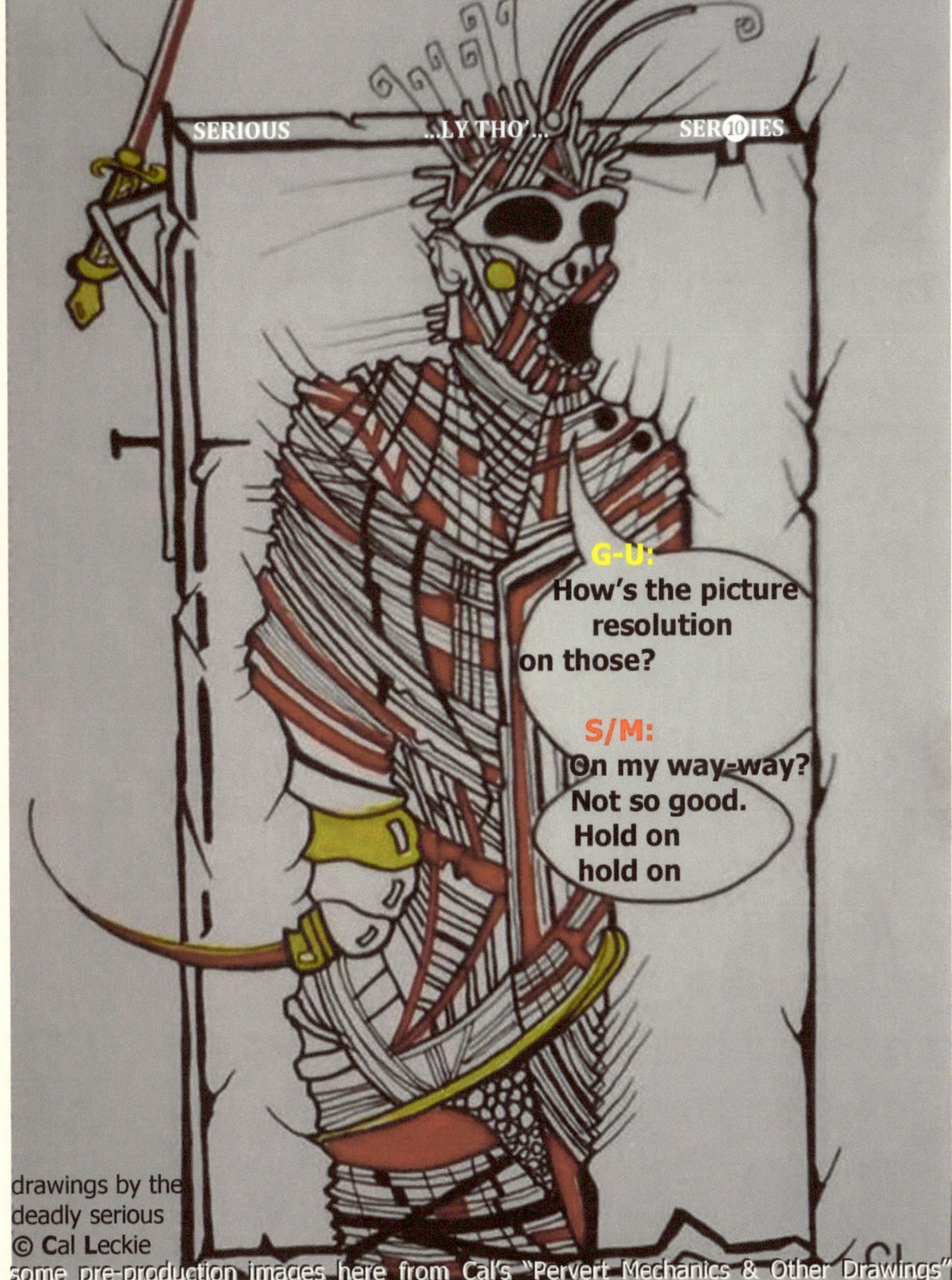

May 13, 2013, Nicholas Thomas Hranilovich phoned in as the shape-shifting_
G-Unit Ronquella to Shawn Misener's *Clutching at Straws* podcast.¯_(ツ)_/¯

SERIOUS   ...LY THO'...   SER10IES

G-U:
How's the picture
resolution
on those?

S/M:
On my way-way?
Not so good.
Hold on
hold on

drawings by the
deadly serious
© Cal Leckie

some pre-production images here from Cal's "Pervert Mechanics & Other Drawings"
Facebook Album are also available in slick format with his own words at Oneiros Books.

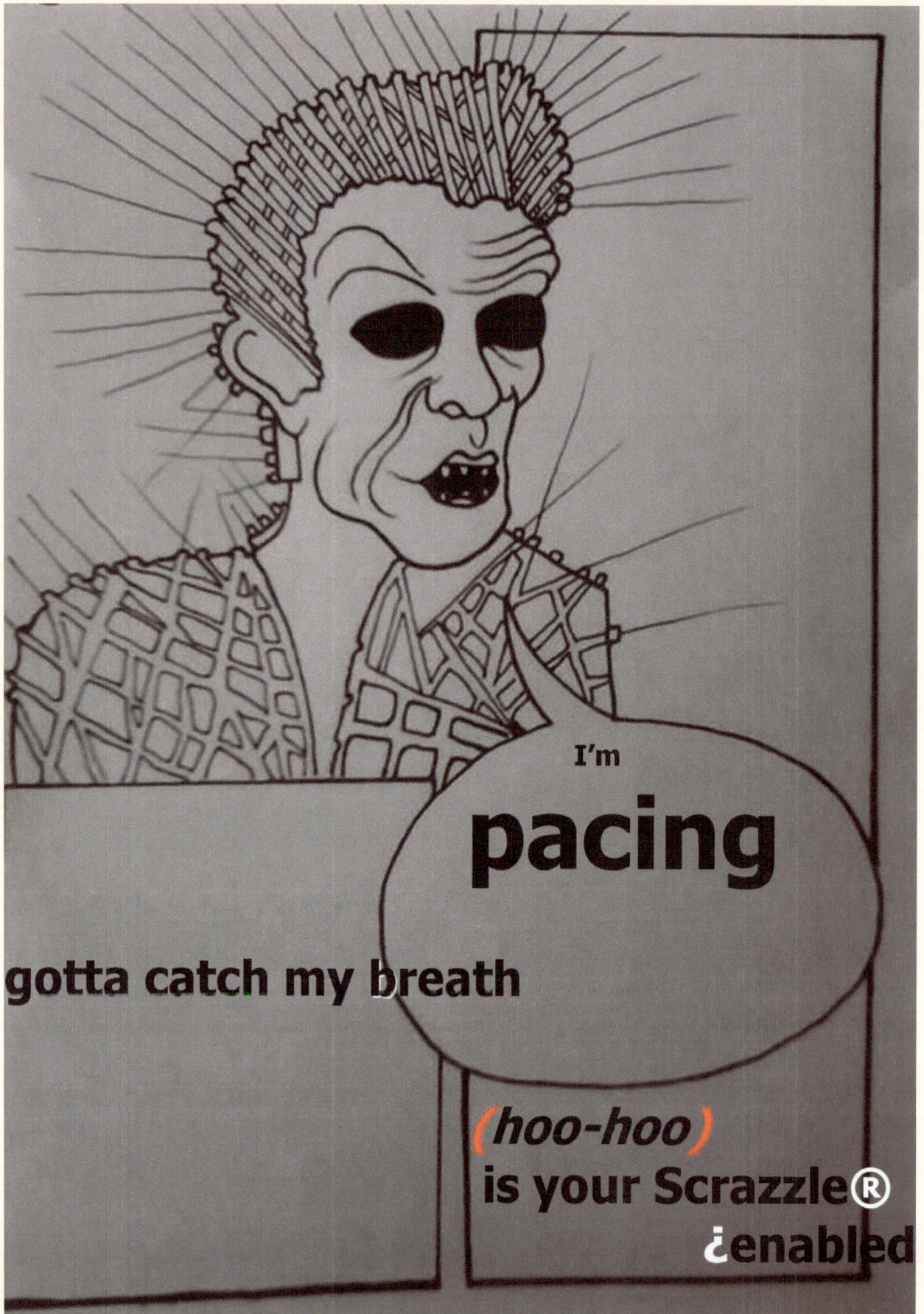

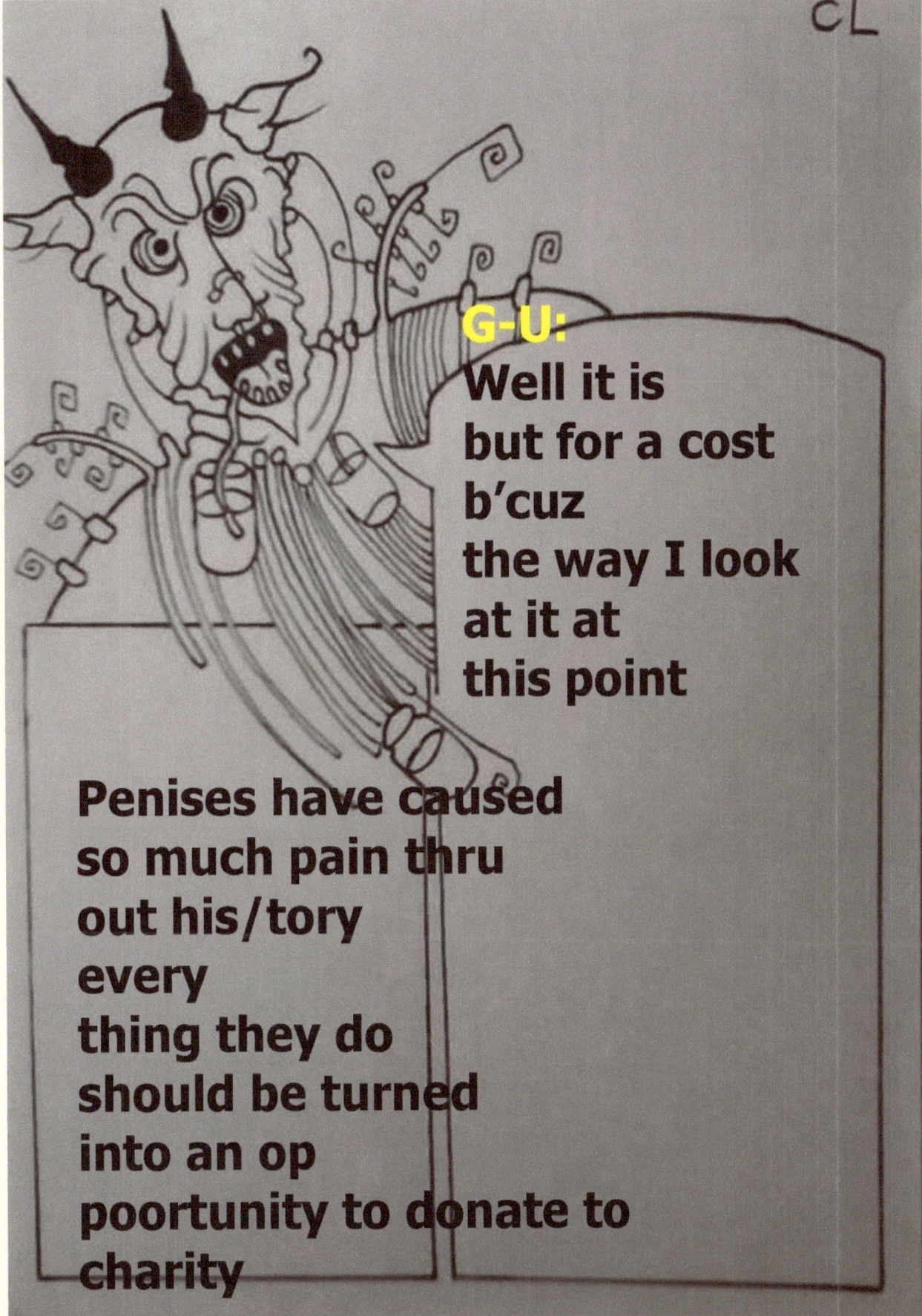

CL

G-U:
Well it is
but for a cost
b'cuz
the way I look
at it at
this point

Penises have caused
so much pain thru
out his/tory
every
thing they do
should be turned
into an op
poortunity to donate to
charity

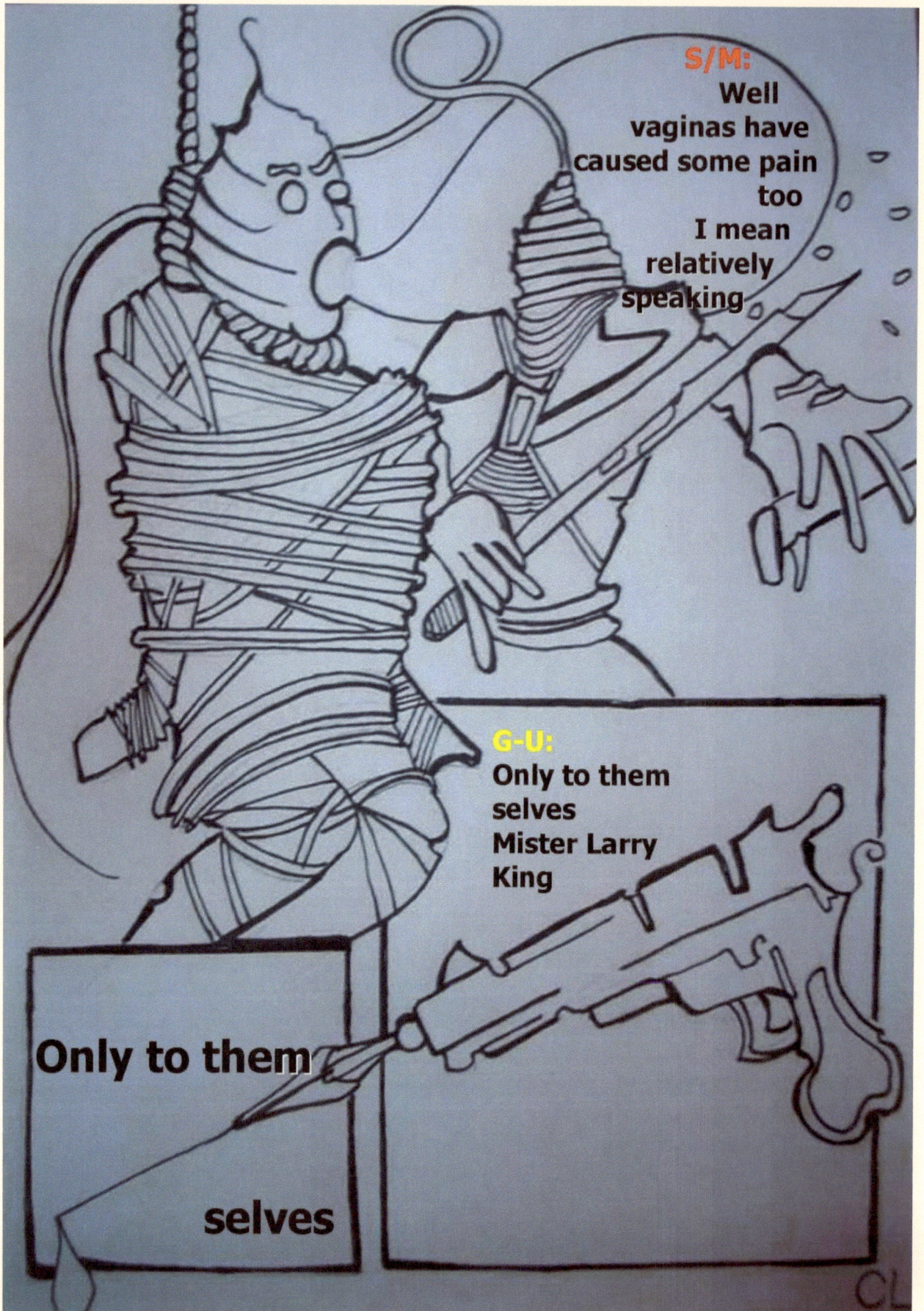

G-U:
The vagina is a self
destructive imploding
star kind of force

it's
constantly roiling
thru patterns
of tumult
like
a hamster

S/M:
Oh?
Explain

wheel of death
where
ever it goes

it is
the Sisyphus of self
hatred

it is
in/
security put
in/
to the form of

two tiny
Velcro
wobbly
bologna
flaps

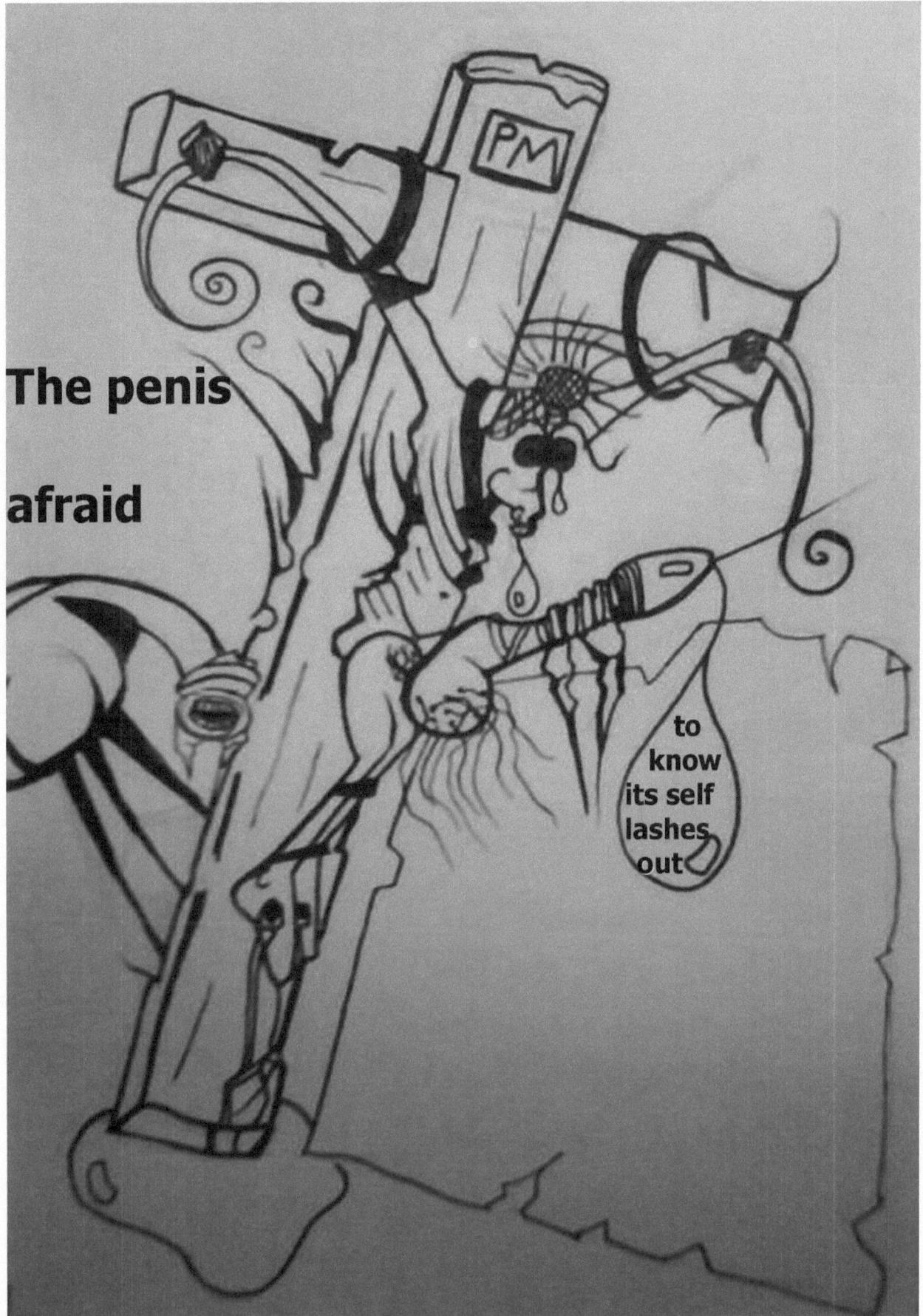

The penis

afraid

PM

to
know
its self
lashes
out

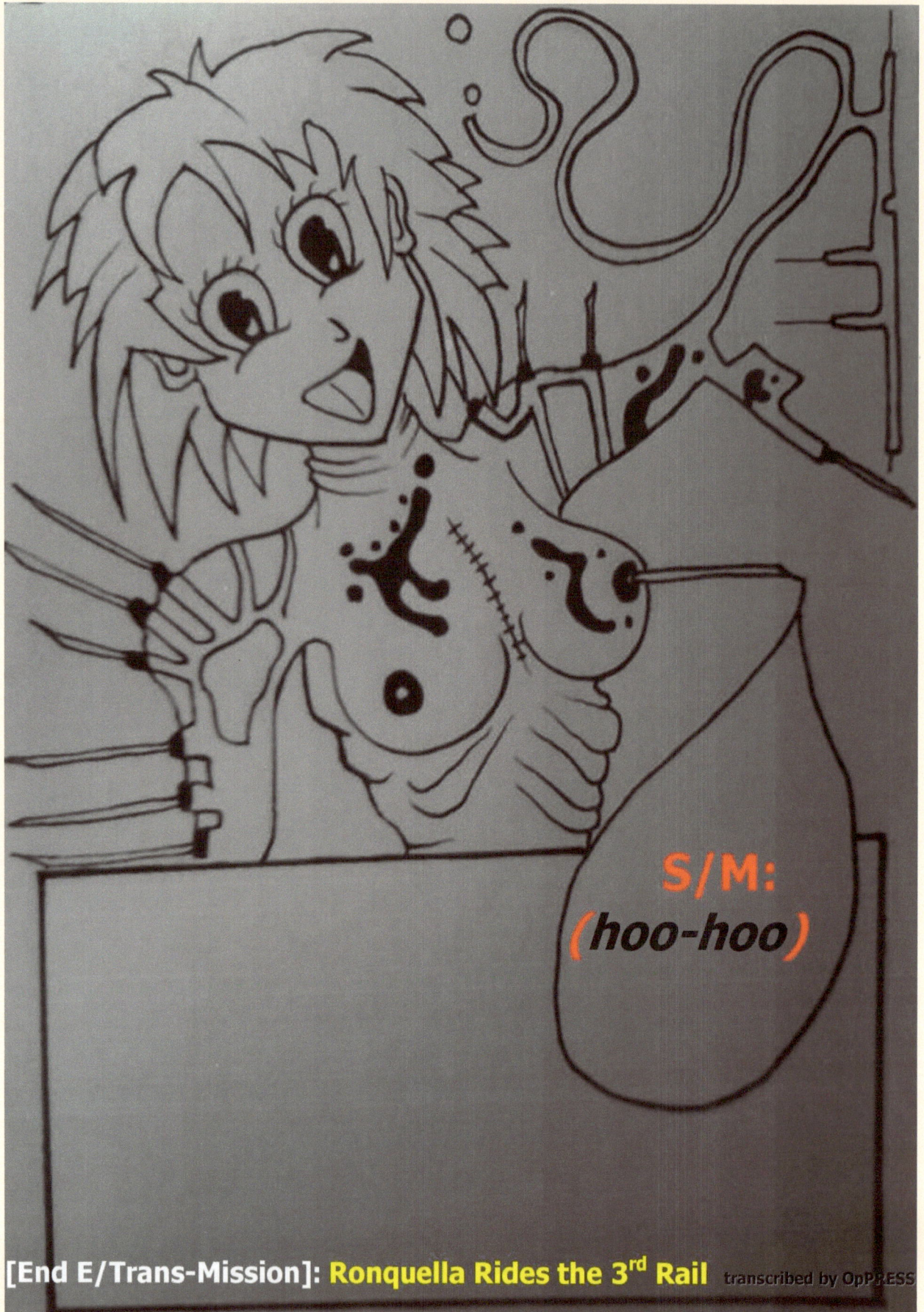

S/M:
(hoo-hoo)

[End E/Trans-Mission]: Ronquella Rides the 3rd Rail   transcribed by OpPRESS

ATOMIC BUSSERY
SERIES <XI> ELEVEN

bus poems by
Reuben©Woolley

back dropped by Ian©Pyper's
"Future Primitive 'Atom' Watercolour Drawings"

lampedusa

'Atom Birds #3'

in the waves
the shadow

i hear the hollow bell

& shall we go
& meet them at the tolling

no flowers
no floating

'Atom Birds 5'

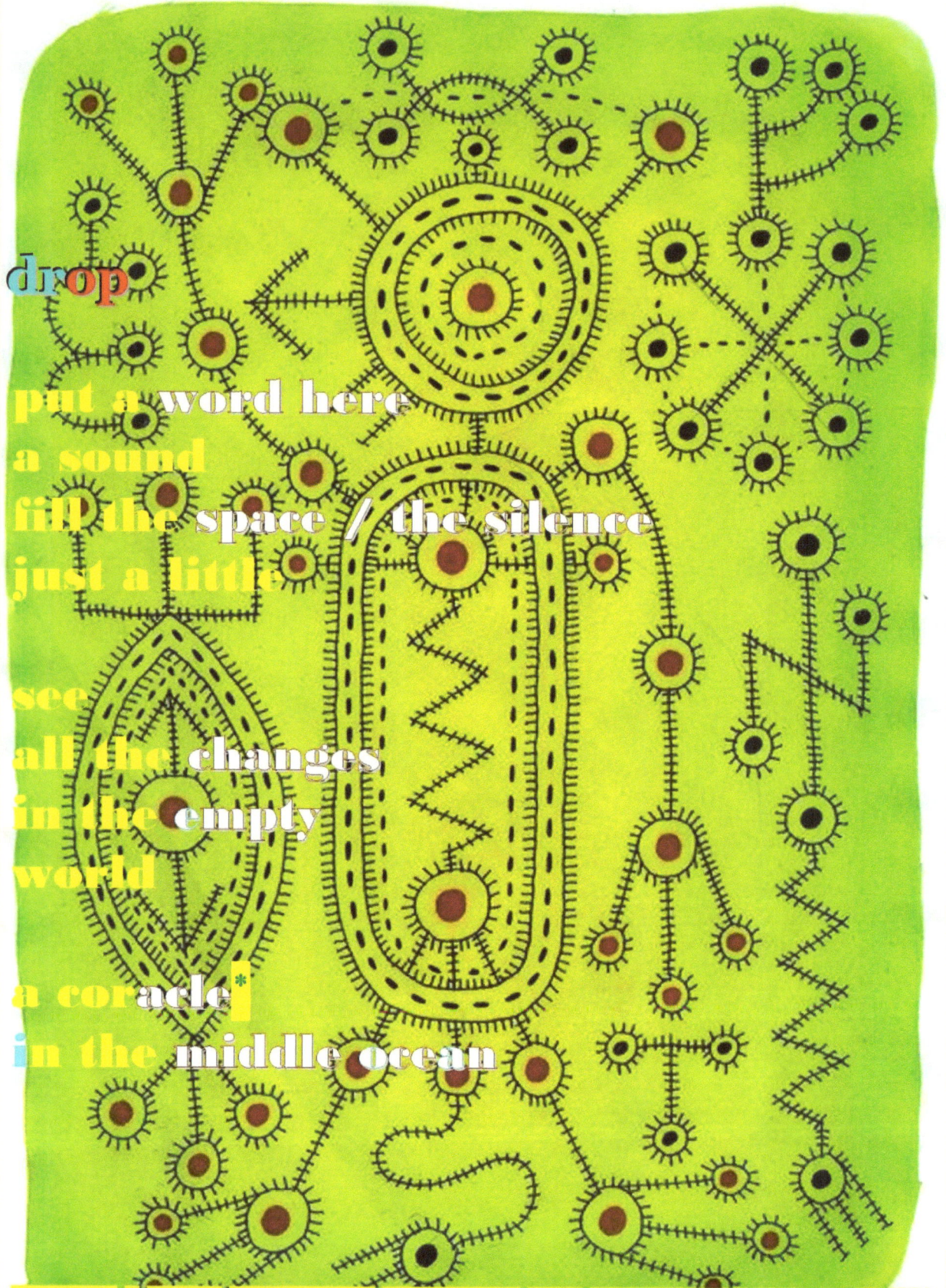

drop

put a word here
a sound
fill the space / the silence
just a little

see
all the changes
in the empty
world

a coracle*
in the middle ocean

*coracle: a small, lightweight, basket-like boat traditionally used in Wales

'Atom Alien (says "hello")'

skins

i hit the land
with all the light i have
[at my]
disposal & the wind
comes for leftovers

nothing's
untouched

my shadow slipped off
downriver

& here i am
quite
naked

i have no shape
to wrap me in
peeled

at the edges

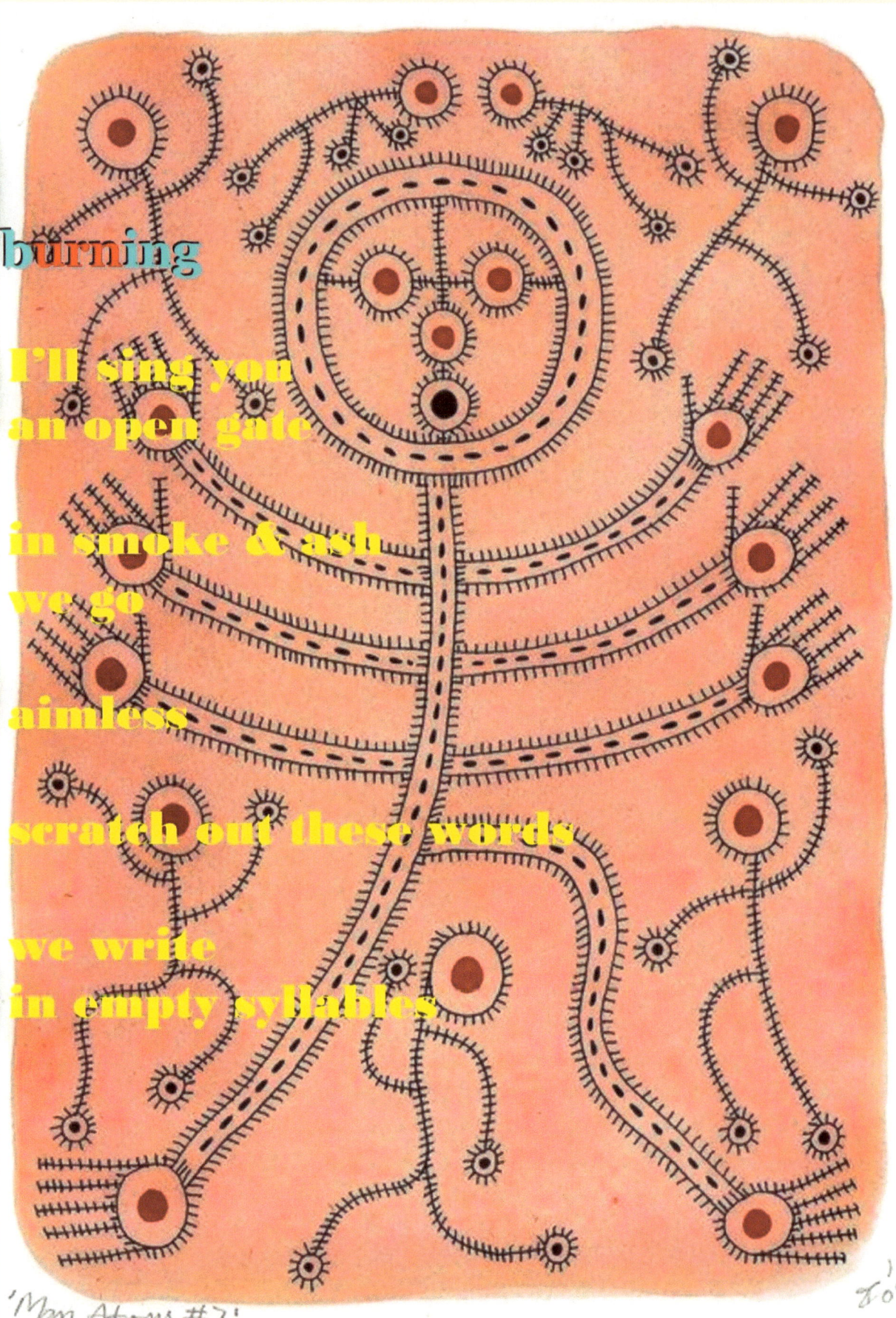

burning

I'll sing you
an open gate

in smoke & ash
we go

aimless

scratch out these words

we write
in empty syllables

'Man Atoms #7'

'8'09

place of residence

let's keep this
simple
like quadrilaterals don't
complicate the view
from all the empty bridges

they tie things
together we wouldn't want
to lose falling

into mudflats & thick
water

crank open
the shutters a reverse
process a little light
on old routines

look
at the grey dust & the spiders hiding
i've lived here before

graved

i make shadows in silence
through the peeling of the hours

in all my mad indifference
the wild time
shining
for wrinkled saints
. dance now

'Dancing the Atom'

cracked face

& my stone laughter

out

careful

in this

last

cold

asking

the broken slabs   & names erased

'Dreaming Through the Atoms'

futures

& this is dark

like wingless moths
do not hit the light

don't die
in ultra-violet

'Little Atom Creature'

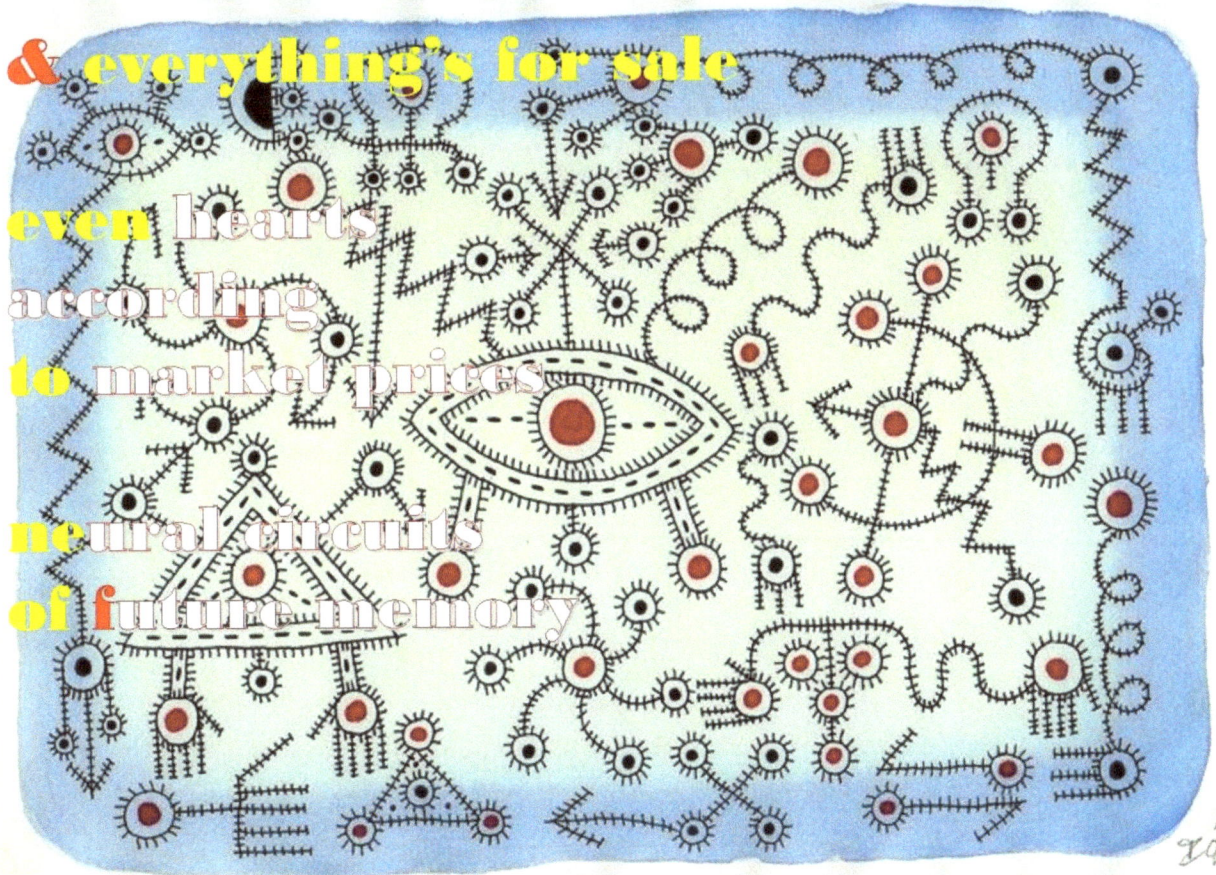

& everything's for sale

even hearts
according
to market prices

neural circuits
of future memory

still swimming

there's always new water
in my hand
however much I never move
it breathes me here
the different spires of bleeding

a sad respiration
of arrivals
and departures

SERIES ☿ 1 2
TRICKSTER

I*N~D#E#X~U*S

Metric Footnotes

[4,21,24,26,27]
~Peer uneasy   <1,2>
        gene yes are test   [4]
    ~All does hucks lea   [51]

[3,4]
V E R S Optych ————————————————————►   <1>
O P~T A T
R E C T Optych ————————————————————►   <1>
I~A N U S
    t h U S   *primus ecco*
CatullU S~t for ass
                                    ▼
    WhilS t the one-verse folds upon itself into Ever
ything   from the outer rim
job   on

[3]
PISS-stem
    ~Mort sac [3,7,18(19),52]   <ii>
        "OK, yes, I'm done. Now
            Get the fork outta my face."

[3,(4),(30)]
Vena sex mock henna
    ~Mz. Dizney Kicks   [3,(5),(9),(13),21,24,(36),(37),40,(45),48,52]
        "For joy for ~Joyce, joy,
            the zebra's in the zygospore,
        ignore, ignore."

[3]
Arrows offer
~Cupidities

[a]
Picks'll loosen
neigh shiss

[3]
Subra-con-chess

[3,4,24,(48),52]
Nigh does
ply exes
a nest of Webstresses

<i,ii,1,2>
[3,5,52]

[3,45,47]
Unique
Ver.sys intechs tal
Disposable Sing Eularity
an artificial black hole-bubble containment≈
reservation barrier buster, rumored

[4]
Fauxto mahn
Taj eerie

[4]
aft terse hex
all any malls
arse add, 'ceptin' wimmin & roosters
~Galen? ~'Stotle? "Greek to me, Offither…

[4]
Rose mar

'een the lines
run aground
~Mel de Ville still bled
slick on open water

[4,(36)]
vie role enfeck shun
ov/en cant asians
sham dial hectic
~El Hombre from outer space

[4,52]
Cask aiding *teh*'s El Lay shun
Ought tawny muss   [4]
          Faint asthma gore ria   [4]

[4]
Avant-Arabesque
          Man I'm beat, *beyond b[ah]roke*   <ii>
     Get back, ~Jack

[5]
Lows Fee lez
     Griff 5th obs *hervé ToRi*
          indie 'hood

[5]
met trick mawn taw jizz   <i,(ii),1>
     ~Eyes in stein

[5]
Sex hundred and sexty-sex daze
     ~*The Beast* sniffs out
          in a moment of quantum lucidity
               an Eroto-comatose cockhorse   [27]
          the golden crack of Dawn
               a flash a smile
          dewy lippity lobe auto me
               studded saddle bustress   [27]
               spur spunk sparkled
                    galloping gooses   [51]
               bobbing buttresses
          take me i'm yours

[5]
cam era
     ob scura
          Universoptychal   [3,4] <1>
     fata
          morgana

[5]
"typer," by
     ~Beershitski

[5,25]

"Dialog Sheet"
[C/S]ession Dynamic
or, How Our No-Mercy Circes Take a Sissy Fuss
Up and Down the Ladder in 6,6,6 Easy Steps [5]
at *Chez Ricochet*, where the caviar, by far [27]

CIR	CLE	ANY	
NO–H	OLE	BAR	[5,25]
RED	TOR	TUR	
ESS	FOR	CED	
FED	PRO	BOS	
CIS	SUS	PEN	[26 (34)]
DED	LAD	DER	
INT	ENS	ORY	
'LEC	TRO	DEV	[(25), (37)]
ICE	HOT	WAX	
VUL	GER	GAG	
ENE	MAS	HUM	[(29)]
BLE	RRR	VIB	
RAT	ORS	PVC	
COR	SET	DEG	[57]
RAD	ATE	SIS	[9,21,33]
TER	ARN	ICA	
NIP	PUL	LEY	[(29)]

80

[6,49]
kick against the pricks
    ~Axe 9:5/26:14

[6]
arse in all Ayn gel
    ~Howlin' Allen aka *Sr. Carlo Marx*

[6]
strict shun nary
    Define me
        DĔG·răd·ĀTE* me   [56]
    *beware; it's in there
                    will be on test

        written onda
[6] Pill whores of Her queue lease:
    neapless ultra   [33]
        "no mo yonda"   [39]

    and yet

[7]
AMAZ♥NE   [Vanity Plated] [49]
    AMAZE ME —   *I mis**read**, so*
        OK, revisionally
    Hanging Is Flying

        whoa, pause all
[7] pausal for the causal

[30]
beet wean
    pissant she 'twere
        bore in,
    say 'sain't ~*Ahh(gusting)*~ so
[7] *bardo 'tain't*
        neither this nor that, here nor there

[7,52]
POW! works change
    top is bottom is top

[7]
Reverse Tricks   <(ii)>
    Ria Grande

[7]

bizz unteen bop
        a sac/ra[('s)peri]mental stopgap   [48]/[10,13,59] <ii>
    ~*Yay, eights!* at 69 still a *play-uh*

[7]

parry shoot — snap-on's a slack
        clapper cincher upper
    come a cute pair annoy ya
        dong alongward

[9]

Fug a dug
        it came in a ~Mailer

[9]

Kühl loud kook [cool &]
    ~*Airist* often knees
    as in ~*Offen* a *Free Lunch*
        not oft
            it's called eliding
    as in gliding a*fore* ward '*st*ead aft
        see: [apos
                sibyl
            trophy]

        Knot yore
    ~Ezekiel Dollar's
Lust Raw   [(5),9,13,21,24,(36),(37),45,(48-9)]
    Of the Metro   [17]

[9,11,13,17,2
Am Anita
    Am Rita
        Am Brosia
            (moosque aria)
        so much rooms, so much
    ~Is a bella, is a sol   <ii>

[9]
bawdy bag   after the insults   ~Catullus
    /*bodhi* bag   *i beg your pardon*   ~Optatianus

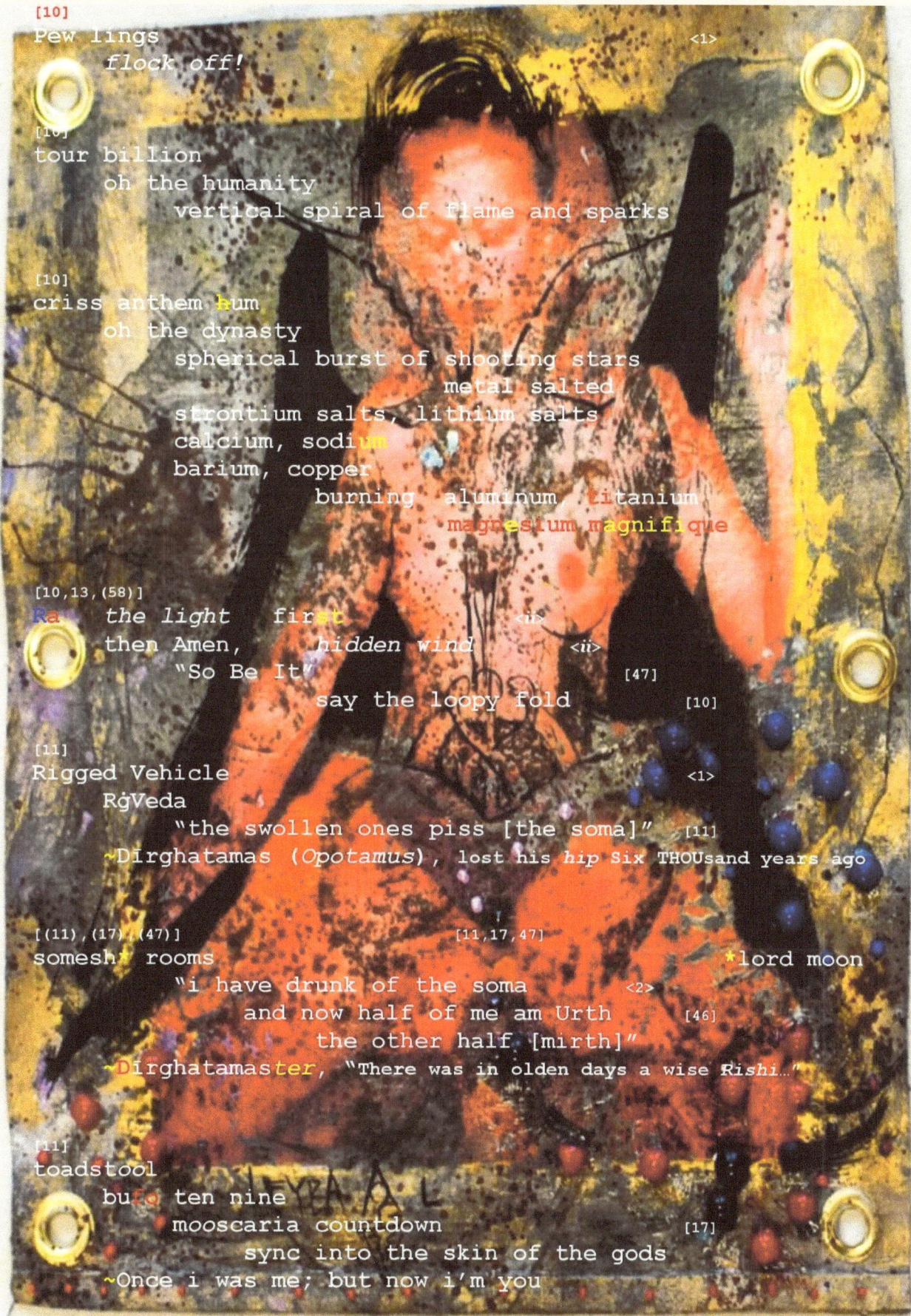

[10]
Pew lings
    flock off!   <1>

[10]
tour billion
    oh the humanity
        vertical spiral of flame and sparks

[10]
criss anthem hum
    oh the dynasty
        spherical burst of shooting stars
                    metal salted
        strontium salts, lithium salts
        calcium, sodium
        barium, copper
            burning aluminum, titanium
                magnesium magnifique

[10,13,(58)]
Ra *the light   first*   <ii>
    then Amen,   *hidden wind*   <ii>
        "So Be It"   [47]
                say the loopy fold   [10]

[11]
Rigged Vehicle   <1>
    RģVeda
    "the swollen ones piss [the soma]" [11]
    ~Dirghatamas (*Opotamus*), lost his *hip* Six THOUsand years ago

[(11),(17),(47)]   [11,17,47]
somesh* rooms   *lord moon
        "i have drunk of the soma   <2>
        and now half of me am Urth   [46]
            the other half [mirth]"
    ~Dirghatamas*ter*, "There was in olden days a wise *Rishi...*"

[11]
toadstool
    bu ten nine
        mooscaria countdown   [17]
            sync into the skin of the gods
    ~Once i was me; but now i'm you

83

[13]
Smiling and everything
        like
    ~Are. Brought-again
        likewise my 7-yr-old at-tension
            captured by the calendared
    '52 Marilyn spread
            up against the wall
        of a cun'tree store slash post or'fice
                        slash arm pit stop
            my 14-yr-old bro,"3-of-5", broke
                his lust to bust my blurted
                            utterance
                    my milkfed innocence
a mobile testes moany all together now   [29]
    back of the wagon
                    comin'round the mountain
            in a buick '59
            '59, buick '59
        yosemite bound   vernal falls
            also naked and celebrated
                a force
            the moral stampede can no more
                shroud
                    in it's dust

    than ~OG Dylan T's green thrust.

[13]
Indus/5
    hundred
        thousand
            millyin yang
    years
        may never know
why 5?
        Hand to god
        Hand that pressed Mohen jo daro
            into delta silt pentagonal
                then swept the lines away
        Hand of ~Arjuna
                too from a litter of 5
        shook as ~Krishna spoke thermo
    maha ha ha
        die damnics

[14]
History Motors
    Indus[ted] like
Kh'mere *you*
      where go?
      all Rouge Lite *like*
Anna's Ozzie
      oh heck
Olmec
      ax'im 'bout
Aksum
      They done.
Men owens?
      Bones. Like
Cucu[ka-choo]teni **and the** Tryp[ptych]illians
      Uncanny ash canny.
      Can't ask the
Nabateans
      — all Petra'fied — what it means.
      Can't ask
Cahokia
      They, too, all up in smoky, *uh,*
      I dream of
My sin eon
      Bronzed like ensconced
Moche
      mole. Can't roll me ova in
Clovis
      starta cultcha — gone way 'fo'
~Sargon was *A cad*
      aeon
          ago. And so
          he too, he's gone, broke
          down the road all *bas*-relieved   *-bah-*
          no hubcaps even   [48]
way gone
          car lot and all.

[15]
Taken/Token from/Old/Bus People
  ~Found Poem/Wall Scrawl, *'81 downtown Sandy Egg-o*

[18]
Transfer(enter fear)ence
  "I am Legion"
      okie tokie, 'Artichokie?   [38]

[(19)]
tooth ishtars
        threw'd iffy cult ease
~Roamin' add age

[21,48]
Cath~urine   the Great*

        catheterize, catheterize
        pull out his "guys"

*"There is nothing, it seems to me, so difficult as to
    escape from that which is essentially agreeable."

        safeword:
[22] Palindrome   [(19),(22),(30),(31),(43),(50)]

        RED NUDE MADAMED UNDER

        or would
[19] Palimpsest be best?
    See, Langwedge [46] is a witch
        that shroomed from a spore from outer space [11]
        man, why we spell out our names to this day 23,60

        or so ~William Tell

            ... what, too soon?

        it's a whole
(40) newer old ardor, baby
    check your ~Buybull [5,6,24,(27),36,37,40,43,45,47,49,(55),56,57,59,61]
        at the door

            ■

        [In the Name of The Square,]

        [The Triangle,]

        [and The Circle.]

        Amen Ra

Typoetics © Mike Castro   PAINtings © Steven Johnson Leyba